Elections, Representation, and Congressional Voting Behavior

Elections, Representation, and Congressional Voting Behavior

The Myth of Constituency Control

Robert A. Bernstein

Texas A&M University

PRENTICE HALL, Englewood Cliffs, New Jersey 07632

Library of Congress Cataloging-in-Publication Data

Bernstein, Robert A. (Robert Alan), (date)
   Elections, representation, and congressional voting behavior: the
myth of constituency control / Robert A. Bernstein.

   Includes bibliography and index
   ISBN 0-13-247792-0
   1. United States Congress—Elections.   2. United States
Congress—Voting.   3. Public opinion—United States.
4. Representative government and representation—United States.
I. Title.
JK1071.B46 1989   88–7899
328.73—dc19   CIP

Editorial/production supervision and
   interior design: Marianne Peters
Cover design: 20/20 Services, Inc.
Manufacturing buyer: Peter Havens

 ©1989 by Prentice-Hall, Inc.
A Division of Simon & Schuster
Englewood Cliffs, New Jersey 07632

Printed in the United States of America
10 9 8 7 6 5 4 3 2 1

ISBN 0-13-247792-0

Prentice-Hall International (UK) Limited, *London*
Prentice-Hall of Australia Pty. Limited, *Sydney*
Prentice-Hall Canada Inc., *Toronto*
Prentice-Hall Hispanoamericana, S.A., *Mexico*
Prentice-Hall of India Private Limited, *New Delhi*
Prentice-Hall of Japan, Inc., *Tokyo*
Simon & Schuster Asia Pte. Ltd., *Singapore*
Editora Prentice-Hall do Brasil, Ltda., *Rio de Janeiro*

To Cindy

Contents

Preface

A *dependence on the people is, no doubt, the primary control on the government.*

James Madison, *Federalist 51*

Americans determined that the members of the legislature should be elected by the people directly, *and for* a very brief term *in order to subject them, not only to the general convictions, but even to the daily passions, of their constituents.*

Alexis DeTocqueville, *Democracy in America*

To what extent do constituencies control the policy choices of their representatives? We know that periodic elections of representatives were intended to force responsiveness of members of Congress to those who elected them—just as lifetime appointments for justices were intended to free members of the court from responsiveness to the wishes of those who selected them. Now, however, "elections are mass popularity contests before a distant and inattentive audience," (Payne, 1977b) and the probability of reelection is well over 0.9 for members of the House of Representatives. Is the intended pattern still in place? This book seeks to determine the extent of constituency control over the policy positions adopted by members of congress once those members have taken office.

I am pleased to thank Cynthia Bernstein, Jon Bond, James Dyer, James Payne, Harvey Tucker, and Arnold Vedlitz for their thoughtful critiques of this work as it developed. I am also grateful to Texas A&M University for a grant that gave me time to think and write.

Some of the data analyzed here were originally collected by the Center for Political Studies of the University of Michigan under a grant from the National Science Foundation.

Of course, none of the aforementioned people or institutions bears any responsibility for the analyses or interpretations presented in this book.

Introduction

For most people, no doubt, elections are seen as the primary mechanism through which common citizens control their government. Elections are, supposedly, the means by which leaders gone astray are replaced by ones more attuned to popular desires.

Robert Weissberg (1976: 170)

Constituents are the most important influence on a Member's voting decision .... Representatives who fail to reflect generally the views of their constituents will soon need other work.

Rep. Lee Hamilton (1987: 228)

There is a deeply entrenched belief in democratic societies that constituencies control the behavior of their representatives. That belief is largely untested but rarely criticized. In the United States, it justifies the use of elections to select members of Congress. As the quotations above illustrate, the belief permeates textbooks and articles on elections, representation, and congressional behavior. In short, the belief that constituencies control the behavior of their representative, especially the behavior of members of Congress, has achieved the status of a myth: "an unproved collective belief that is accepted uncritically and is used to justify a social institution" (Random House, 1967).

The myth dates back at least to the eighteenth century when such authors as Bentham, Mill, Hamilton, and Madison were arguing for frequent elections to assure the dependency of legislators on their constituents.[1] Pitkin (1967: 201) summarizes their position as the now "familiar notion"

> that officeholders want to be reelected, and hence will do what the voters want; elections make it to their interest to further the voters' interest.

Assumptions regarding the truth of the myth underlie the nineteenth-century warnings by DeTocqueville and Mill of the "tyranny of the majority." As Pomper (1980: 28) argues, "majority tyranny can only be a threat if the majority in elections makes policy."

The broad outlines of the myth are assumed to be true by modern theorists who argue for "one man, one vote." As Dixon (1968) notes, unless one assumes that representatives are acting as delegates of their constituencies, "there would seem to be little reason to worry about the mathematics of district population regarding representation" (p. 191). Similarly, modern theorists are accepting at least the broad outlines of the myth when they assume that representatives' issue positions will influence their reelection prospects. As Davis, Hinich, and Ordeshook (1970) argue, if the electorate is "neither attentive nor responsive" to representatives' issue positions, there is no value in all of the theoretical work on spatial analysis of voting.

The myth is fundamental to some of the standard works on Congress and elections. MacNeil (1963: 451) contends that a U.S. Representative "could violate the sensibilities and the views of his constituents only at the imminent peril of being forced into political retirement." Davidson and Oleszek (1981: 386) state that

> Representatives' actions are constrained also by the threat of defeat. Occasionally members voice policies or views at odds with those of their district's voters; often (but not always) incumbents subsequently shift their stands to retain their seats.

Pomper (1980: 221) claims that when representatives "see a conflict between the demands of their constituency, their party, and their own views...their vote is for the constituency interest." Erikson and Wright (1985: 103) bluntly state that "constituencies tend to reward and punish incumbents on the basis of their policy positions." Even the most up-to-date and widely-used texts are not exempt from perpetuation of the myth. The only article on determinants of congressional voting in the 1987 Congressional Quarterly reader (Davidson and Oleszek, ed.) is Representative Hamilton's defense of the myth that constituents control the voting behavior of their representatives.

The myth of constituency control goes largely unchallenged by supporters of democracy because democrats desperately want the myth to be true.[2] If constituencies do not control their representatives, if representatives are basically free to vote for whatever policies they think best, what then is the argument for having a democracy?

As Pomper (1980) contends, there is nothing about the democratic selection process, that is, nothing about elections, that suggests that democracy will produce the wisest or most capable rulers. And there are good reasons for expecting that elections will produce status-driven, shallow-thinking representatives (Payne, 1977b).

Why, then, should we elect rulers? Why not select them by lot? Or by examination? Or by some other means? Proponents of democracy are almost forced to respond that we ought to elect representatives so that the government will do our bidding, not the bidding of those who rule: it is via elections that we get a government "of the people, by the people, and for the people." As Pomper (1980: 30) puts it,

> Elections...by their very existence...act as a restraint on government and tend to bring representatives to further the needs and wants of their constituents.

Lending credence to the myth is its very simplicity. The logic behind constituency control can be summarized in the following syllogism:

MAJOR PREMISE: representatives want to be reelected.

MINOR PREMISE: constituencies are likely to reelect only those representatives who have supported policies favored by their constituencies.

CONCLUSION: representatives have no choice but to support policies that their constituencies favor.

The reasoning is straightforward; the premises, sensible.

Then, too, the myth is comforting—especially to those who want to see democracy succeed but are depressed with the quality of the people elected to public office. They can always reassure themselves that the quality or morality of members of Congress is not too important. Presumably, even dim-witted or corrupt members want to get reelected. They, no less (and perhaps more) than the brilliant and honest members, will fear voter retaliation, and will translate the people's wishes into law.

The myth of constituency control is also appealing in offering excuses to those who do not pay quite as much attention to public affairs as they think they ought to. If Joe Public did not pay too much attention to how his representative voted on a House bill yesterday, that was presumably O.K. The myth suggests that, in casting his vote, the representative had to worry about it later being used as a campaign issue, so the representative had to vote as the public would have wanted, regardless of whether the public was aware of the vote at the time it was cast. Similarly, if Jane Public did not pay too much attention to who was running for Congress, that too was O.K. The myth tells us that whoever gets elected will have to do what his or her constituents want, so why be concerned over a lapse in citizen duty?

Put simply, we want to believe that representatives vote the will of their constituents. It's nice to have a simple myth that justifies our form of government, soothes our dissatisfaction with the quality of public officials, and excuses our failures to perform our duties as citizens.

Unfortunately, wanting something to be true does not make it so. The myth has been subject to very little empirical investigation. As with most myths, there is probably an element of truth in the myth of constituency control. But, how much of an element—particularly with regard to constituency control of Congress? That is the question this book seeks to answer.

ORGANIZATION OF THE BOOK

The first chapter lays out the logic that undergirds the myth. It details the assumptions and hypotheses regarding citizens, constituencies, and members of Congress that can be verified, partially verified, or falsified by the evidence we have from surveys, election results, and congressional voting behavior. The following three chapters present and evaluate the evidence: chapter 2, the evidence regarding citizens; chapter 3, the evidence regarding constituencies; and chapter 4, the evidence regarding members of Congress. The concluding chapter discusses the implications of the findings and suggests possible changes in the electoral system.[3]

NOTES

[1]For detailed discussion of their positions, see Pitkin (1967) and Birch (1971).

[2]It does not go entirely unchallenged. Among social scientists questioning the myth are Weissberg (1976), Stone (1980), Luttbeg (1981), Maass (1983), and Wayman (1983). Normative political scientists, from both sides of the political spectrum, have argued that the myth is not true.

[3]As this book calls into question the empirical basis for the myth, every effort will be made to gather and interpret evidence so as to uncover as much support for the myth as is possible. If this study finds little empirical support for the myth, there simply is not very much to be found.

ONE

The Logic behind the Myth

This chapter examines the logic behind the myth of constituency control as it applies to Congress. The objectives are to lay out the assumptions and hypotheses underlying the myth and to identify those that can be tested empirically.

As stated in the Introduction, the syllogism underlying the myth begins with the major premise that members of Congress want to be reelected. Clearly, that premise does not apply to all members of Congress. Every term there are a few who plan to retire. There may also be a few who do not much care whether they are reelected. Certainly, there are at least anecdotal reports to that effect (Kennedy, 1956; Mayhew, 1974; Payne, et al., 1984). Still, it does not seem worthwhile to try empirically to test the major premise. Almost all members of Congress do stand for reelection, and it seems fair to assume that, for all but a handful, reelection is a strong motivating force—either as an end in itself, or as a means to achieve other ends.[1]

Acknowledging the validity of the major premise does not concede the validity of the myth. We could "... conjure up a vision of United States congressmen as single-minded seekers of reelection ..." (Mayhew, 1974: 5) and still not accept the conclusion that members have to support policies favored by their constituents. There are assumptions underlying

1

the minor premise and the conclusion of the syllogism that have to be detailed and tested before we can evaluate how much truth the myth is built upon.

The minor premise can be restated as the following hypothesis:

> Controlling for other variables, the more the policies voted for by the incumbent deviate from those favored by his or her constituency, the lower the probability that the incumbent will get reelected.

Let's first look at the assumptions regarding citizens that undergird that hypothesis.[2]

ASSUMPTIONS REGARDING CITIZENS

Citizen Knowledge

The first assumption is that citizens have sufficient knowledge to exercise control:

a. that citizens can distinguish the candidate who is the incumbent from the candidate(s) who is (are) not, and

b. that citizens can distinguish the policies that the incumbent has supported from those that he or she has not supported.

Citizens must know who the incumbents are in order to reward or punish them. Citizens do not have to be able to recall incumbents' names. They do not even have to be able to recognize the name of their incumbent from a list of names. But they do have to be able to distinguish the incumbent from his or her opponent(s) *given both the name and party of all candidates in the race.* In the voting booth, citizens are given the name and party of each candidate. If they cannot distinguish the incumbent given that information, they cannot reward or punish the incumbent for his or her behavior in office.

This knowledge might not be necessary in a nation with tightly-controlled, policy-oriented parties. In those nations, the legislator is a person who rubber-stamps party policy. Voters can control policy by rewarding or punishing the party, regardless of who their personal representatives are. But in the United States, where members of Congress from the same party can have opposing policy stances, it is necessary to know who a member is in order to reward or punish him or her for a policy stance.

Citizens must also know what the incumbent's policies have been. The threat to retaliate against those who adopt unpopular policy positions is not credible if the policy positions are unknown. Similarly, citizens cannot reelect those who have supported popular policies unless they know *what* policies have been supported.

Must every citizen know every policy position taken by his or her representative for there to be constituency control? Perhaps not, but constituency control cannot be exerted by those who do not know, at least in a general way, how the incumbent has voted. Nor can constituency control extend to those issues on which only a small percentage of the constituents know how the incumbent has voted.

Surely, if only 10% of the constituents know how the incumbent has voted on a particular issue, it is not necessary for the incumbent to support either the majority position held by the 10% or the majority position held in the district in order to get reelected. But even if most of the constituents know how the incumbent has voted on every issue, and even if all who know vote on the basis of that knowledge, it is still possible that the incumbent who has adopted unpopular positions will be reelected.

For example, suppose that 60% of the voters know how the incumbent has voted on military spending. Let's call them the informed electorate. Suppose further that only 40% of the electorate and 40% of the informed electorate approved of the position the incumbent has taken. Consequently, only 40% of the informed electorate (24% of all voters) would vote for the incumbent; the other 60% of the informed electorate (36% of the whole electorate) would oppose the incumbent. That losing margin among the informed electorate is not enough to ensure the defeat of the incumbent. The incumbent could still get reelected with sufficient support from the uninformed electorate. Support from over 65% of the uninformed electorate (over 26% of the whole electorate), combined with the minority support from the informed electorate, would be enough to win.

If by constituency control we mean the condition in which the member of Congress must vote as the majority wants on every issue, that condition will exist only if every citizen knows the incumbent's vote on every issue. If, however, by constituency control we mean simply that the probability is very high that on any issue the member will vote as the majority of his or her constituents want, then citizen control can exist with more limited knowledge.

Clearly, the lower the percentage of knowledgeable constituents and the lower the percentage of bills or general policy stances about which they have knowledge, the less likely policy deviation from the constituency will determine the fate of a reelection effort.

It is hard to know what constitutes the minimum knowledge of the incumbent's policies sufficient to exercise control. To tightly control the behavior of the representative, citizens would have to know the representative's positions on specific issues. To exercise a looser sort of control, it is probably sufficient that citizens have a general notion as to how liberal or conservative the incumbent's voting has been. Citizens who know that their representative is a "liberal" or an "extreme conservative" probably have enough knowledge to exercise at least loose control over the representative. Citizens who do not know even the general ideological position taken by their representative do not have enough knowledge to exercise even loose control.

Willingness to Reward and Punish

Knowledge of how the incumbent has voted is not enough to sustain the hypothesis embodied in the minor premise. Citizens must prefer the adoption of some policies to the adoption of others, and they must vote to reward incumbents who voted as the citizens wanted and to punish those who did not vote as they wanted.

If citizens vote on the basis of who is the most photogenic candidate (as many may have in the 1960 presidential race), or on the basis of concerns other than policy differences, we cannot expect the hypothesis to hold. Reelection prospects will depend upon policy differences and constituency control will exist only if substantial percentages of the citizens use the vote to reward those who have adopted popular policies and to punish those who have adopted unpopular policies. Rewards and punishments at the voting booth are supposed to keep members of Congress in line. If citizens fail to vote on policy lines, representatives need not adopt popular policies.

There are a number of reasons why citizens might not vote on policy lines. First, citizens may wish to defer to the representative's judgment. Some voters may think that the members representing them in Congress are better trained and more informed than they are themselves. If a significant percentage of the electorate is deferential on issues, there can be no constituency control.

Second, citizens may not vote on the basis of policy differences if they expect that they would have had even greater differences with a representative from the other major party. To the extent that observed deviation is tolerated because that deviation is the least that can be expected, constituencies lose control over their representatives.

Third, policy deviation may not be as important to the constituency as other actions taken by the representative. Constituencies may be especially forgiving of policy deviation by representatives who intervene in the government bureaucracy on their behalf (Fiorina, 1977a, 1977b; Fenno, 1978; Johannes, 1984; Parker, 1987; Larson, 1987). To the extent that work on their constituents' behalf insulates incumbents from punishment on policy grounds, constituencies lose control over the policy positions adopted by their representatives.

Finally, citizens may base their voting on personal characteristics of the incumbent or of his or her opponent, rather than on the incumbent's policy stances. For example, a citizen might fail to vote for a dishonest or immoral incumbent, even if that incumbent had voted for issues that the citizen favored. A citizen might vote for an honest or virtuous incumbent, even if that incumbent had voted for positions that the citizen opposed. Citizens might vote for or against an incumbent because of his or her religion, sex, race, marital status, social class, and so on. The higher the percentage of votes cast for other than policy reasons, the harder it is to maintain constituency control.

Even if constituents are not deferential, and even if they try to vote on the basis of policy differences, it is to some degree impossible for them to reward and punish incumbents for their policy stances. Citizens have two choices: to reelect or defeat the incumbent. If the incumbent supported some popular and some unpopular policies, the constituency must either reward deviation or punish loyalty. Even a perfectly informed constituency with preferences on all issues will have to vote for some incumbents with whom they disagree on some issues—or else vote against some incumbents with whom they agree on some issues. With one vote, citizens cannot simultaneously reward and punish incumbent voting on all issues. As a consequence, it is unrealistic to expect constituency control over members of Congress on every issue.

Given a measure of perceived distance between the general policy preferences of each citizen and the policies adopted by his or her representative, it is possible to estimate the willingness of citizens to reward and punish on the basis of policy differences. Controlling for other factors, willingness to reward is shown by the percentage voting for reelection among those whose policy preferences are near those adopted by the incumbent. Willingness to punish is shown by the percentage voting against reelection among those whose policy preferences are far from those adopted by the representative. To the extent that voters are not rewarding representatives who are close to them on policy issues and punishing those who are far away, the probability of constituency control diminishes.

Summary

The minor premise in the syllogism underlying the myth of constituency control—that increased policy deviation from the constituency lowers the probability of a representative's reelection—is logically derived from assumptions regarding citizen behavior. Those assumptions, regarding citizen knowledge and willingness to reward and punish on the basis of policy differences, can be investigated empirically. The smaller the percentage of citizens with both the knowledge and the willingness to reward and punish, the lower the probability that increased policy deviation by the representative will affect the outcome of a reelection bid.

ASSUMPTIONS REGARDING CONSTITUENCIES

It should be noted that even if the logic supporting the minor premise cannot be empirically substantiated, the minor premise itself might be so substantiated. In other words, it is possible that incumbents who have voted for unpopular policies are likely to suffer defeat for reasons other than those stated above. For example, in supporting unpopular policies they may tend to alienate elites who share policy preferences with most other constituents, and those elites may finance opposition in primaries or general elections, decreasing the incumbent's reelection prospects. Similarly, incumbents supporting popular policies might tend to be reelected for reasons other than those stated above. For example, incumbents supporting popular policies may get more media coverage than those supporting unpopular policies. That increased media coverage might increase reelection prospects.

It is also possible that a small percentage of the citizens with the knowledge and willingness to act as the myth suggests is decisive in reelection races. A small minority that does behave in accordance with the mythology can determine election outcomes when the rest of the electorate is divided. This may occur often enough so that reelection prospects would tend to vary inversely with the policy distance between the representative and his or her constituency as a whole.

Even some of the most ardent proponents of constituency control admit that citizens do not individually behave as the myth would suggest. They nevertheless contend that constituencies as a whole behave in a manner that exercises control over their representatives (see, for example, Wright, 1978). It is possible for constituencies to reward and punish policy deviation even if the overwhelming majority of citizens do not themselves reward or punish deviation. Therefore, it is necessary to test the minor premise, the hypothesis linking deviation from constituency preference to probability of defeat, even if the assumptions regarding citizen knowledge and willingness to reward and punish cannot be substantiated.

Measures can be constructed of the policy distance between representatives and their constituencies. If those measures are not related to the probability of reelection defeat, the probability decreases that constituencies control the behavior of their representatives.

ASSUMPTIONS REGARDING MEMBERS OF CONGRESS

The myth of constituency control assumes that members of Congress *are forced* to respond to the rewards and punishments of the voting booth. That conclusion does not automatically follow even if the first two premises are valid.

First, members of Congress may desire reelection but still desire something more than reelection. For example, a member might endanger his or her chances for reelection in order to do what he thinks is best for the nation.[3]

Second, even if citizens do act to reward and punish policy stances, members of Congress might not believe that they do. On some or all issues, some members may believe that nobody back home cares how they vote. Members with seniority or with a successful "home style" might be especially likely to feel that they can deviate from what their constituencies want and still get reelected (Kingdon, 1973; Fenno, 1978; Parker, 1987; Larson, 1987).

Third, a member of Congress might be unable to determine his or her constituency's opinion on a policy. Or the member might misread public opinion. The member might vote against public opinion, thinking he or she was voting with it (Maass, 1983).

Under any of these three circumstances, the first two premises underlying the myth might be valid but the conclusion invalid.

To further complicate matters, the conclusion might be correct even if the reasoning leading up to it is faulty. Members of Congress might submit to constituency control even if they do not have to. For example, members might vote as their constituents wish because they fear voter retaliation, even if those fears are unfounded. Or members might feel that they *ought* to vote their constituents' wishes, even if they thought such voting would not affect their reelection prospects (Luttbeg, 1981).

Whether members of Congress vote as their constituencies wish because of a well-founded fear of voter retaliation, because of a poorly-founded fear of retaliation, or because of democratic zeal, there is still constituency control. Therefore, regardless of whether citizens or constituencies reward and punish incumbents based on their policy positions, it is important to test separately whether members of Congress *behave* as though they were controlled by their constituents.

Distinguishing Control from Coincidence

In testing the validity of the conclusion, it is important that we do not confuse coincidence in policy positions by representatives and constituencies with *control* over the representatives' policies by the constituencies. As a number of authors have noted, representatives may vote as constituencies wish because they feel they must, but they may also vote as constituencies wish because they share the same values (Zeigler and Tucker, 1978; Luttbeg, 1981; McCrone and Stone, 1986). Therefore, to demonstrate the existence of constituency control, it is not sufficient merely to demonstrate a coincidence in policy positions between representatives and their constituencies.

It is to be expected that representatives and constituents will favor the same policies more often than not. After all, the representative comes from the same geographic area as his or her constituents, and has been elected to Congress by those constituents. We should not be surprised if a Harlem representative is anti-segregationist or if a Detroit representative favors restrictions on auto imports. Those representatives may simply be voting their own opinions, opinions that coincide with the opinions of 80% or more of their constituents.

As Stone (1980: 400) argues, the difference between policy coincidence and policy control is especially critical in determining whether representatives will be responsive to changes in constituency demands over time:

> If constituency-representative policy agreement results from the sharing of policy preferences without active influence or responsiveness, the constituency retains no mechanism for assuring continued policy agreement ... [I]f constituency opinion changes, members may be markedly out of step with their constituencies ...

The critical research question is whether "congressional elections compel representatives to respond to constituency opinion" (p. 404).

The key to distinguishing between coincidence and control is to observe members of Congress when there is a difference between their own opinions and the opinions of their constituents. In instances where the members' own ideology (or party or presidential pressures) would suggest casting one vote, while constituency pressures would suggest casting another, which way do members actually vote? Only if members tend to bow to constituency wishes in those instances can we conclude that there is constituency *control*.

CHAPTER SUMMARY

This chapter has examined the logic behind the myth of constituency control to find assumptions and hypotheses that can be tested empirically. At the heart of that logic is the premise that only those members of Congress who support policies favored by their constituencies are likely to be reelected, and the conclusion that members of Congress, desiring reelection, have no choice but to support those policies that their constituencies favor.

Behind the premise are two assumptions regarding citizens: (1) that citizens' knowledge of their representatives and the policies supported by those representatives is sufficiently widespread so that control is possible, and (2) that citizens' willingness to reward and punish on the basis of policy distance from the representative is sufficiently widespread so that control is actualized by influencing the representative's reelection prospects.

To verify the logic behind the premise, support has to be shown for both assumptions. Hence, verification of the logic underlying the premise will require demonstrations that there is widespread knowledge of both incumbents and their policies, and a widespread willingness to vote on the basis of policy agreement or disagreement with the incumbent. If citizens behave as the myth of constituency control would suggest, it should be possible to demonstrate that for a substantial percentage of citizens, the probability of voting to reelect significantly decreases as the policy distance between citizen and representative widens.

Even proponents of the idea of constituency control acknowledge the difficulty of finding empirical support for the assumptions regarding citizen behavior. However, proponents are quick to point out that the premise relating policy deviation to reelection prospects could be true for constituencies as a whole, even if the assumptions regarding individual citizens are not true. If constituencies behave as the myth would suggest, it should be possible to demonstrate support for the hypothesis that the more the policies voted for by the incumbent deviate from those favored by his or her constituency, the lower the probability that the incumbent will be reelected.

The ultimate test of whether there is empirical support for the myth lies in an examination of the behavior of the members of Congress. When conflicts arise between the dictates of the members' ideologies and the dictates of their constituencies, how do they vote? Even if neither individual citizens nor constituencies as a whole behave as the myth suggests, if members of Congress behave as though they are controlled by their constituencies, then the myth has all the support it needs. If members do not behave as though they are controlled, then the myth cannot be substantiated.

Since that is where the ultimate test must be made, it is tempting to move directly to examine the behavior of members of Congress. But that could prove unsatisfying without examining citizen and constituency behavior. Especially if members did not vote as though they were under substantial constituency control, one would want to know why they did not behave as the myth would suggest. By first looking at the behavior of citizens and constituencies, it is possible to determine the likelihood of electoral reward and punishment. That likelihood would tend to affect the extent to which members allowed themselves to be controlled. It is true that the behavior of members is theoretically separable from that of citizens and constituents: members may tend to ignore constituencies' policy preferences, even if ignoring those preferences leads to electoral retaliation; and members may tend to bow to constituencies' preferences, even if bowing to those preferences has no effect on reelection prospects. However, the evidence would be much more convincing if it showed a consistent pattern: citizens, constituencies, and members all behaving as the myth would suggest;

or neither citizens, constituencies, nor members behaving as the myth would suggest.

NOTES

[1]For a detailed examination of this premise, see Mayhew (1974).

[2]The assumptions differ from those listed by Weissberg (1976); but his focus is on selection of representatives for future congresses, mine on reelection of incumbents.

[3]For specific instances where this happened, see Kennedy (1956). Payne, et al., (1984) describe "program types" who might be expected to act in this fashion.

TWO

Assumptions Regarding Citizens

This chapter investigates the empirical support for assumptions underlying the premise that citizens reward and punish incumbents based on how those incumbents have voted. To carry out such an investigation requires information about the knowledge, preferences, motivations, and behavior of citizens.

DATA SOURCES AND LIMITATIONS

It is not as easy as it might seem to get that sort of information. Researchers cannot get inside people's heads, nor can they tell by simple observation people's knowledge, preferences, motivations, or voting behavior. They are pretty much forced to ask people how much they know, how they feel, why they voted as they did, and for whom they voted.

Those questions are asked in the surveys conducted each election year by the Center for Political Studies (CPS) at the University of Michigan. The 1978-1984 CPS surveys, made available by the Inter-University Consortium for Political and Social Research, form the basis for the analysis in this chapter.

While analysis of the CPS surveys is "state of the art" so far as political science is concerned, it is important to be aware of the restrictions placed on the analysis by those surveys, the relevant weaknesses in the surveys, and the bias such weaknesses tend to introduce into the analysis.

The most obvious restriction on the analysis is that answers can only be found to questions that were asked by the Michigan researchers. For the purposes of this analysis, other questions might have been preferred; but the analysis must make do with what the Michigan researchers have reported.

All survey research has weaknesses related to getting people to respond to the survey in the first place, and getting them to give valid answers in the second (Bernstein and Dyer, 1984). The CPS surveys are no exception. Some people refuse to be interviewed. For various reasons, some people cannot be interviewed. The CPS has generally been successful in getting completed interviews from only about 70%-75% of those they have tried to interview. There is no way of knowing whether those who are interviewed differ in important ways from those who are not interviewed. However, it seems likely that those who know less about politics are less willing to be interviewed than are those who know more. If so, information from the surveys might, for example, overstate the percentage of the citizens who can recognize the name or party of their representative.

It is clear that the answers respondents give are not always valid. Those being interviewed have a tendency to say things that will please the interviewer. To some extent this explains why some claim to have voted when they, in fact, did not. Attempts to please the interviewer may also lead citizens to state opinions on issues or candidates that they have not thought much about (Converse, 1964).

Special circumstances in 1980 and 1984 further suggest that results from those surveys may not reflect the knowledge and opinions of citizens in general. In presidential election years, including 1980 and 1984, the CPS surveys incorporate both pre- and postelection interviews. The preelection interviews might have stimulated an interest in politics and the election that otherwise would not have been there. Such an interest could have made the postelection sample more politically knowledgeable and opinionated than the general public.

BIAS

The restrictions and weaknesses of the CPS surveys are likely to introduce bias into the analysis. All such bias is likely to favor the assumptions regarding citizen knowledge and willingness to reward and punish on the basis of policy differences.

To the extent that the CPS samples are unrepresentative of the population, they probably overrepresent politically active, interested, knowledgeable citizens (Clausen, 1968-69). The samples underrepresent those who are embarrassed about how little they know of politics, those who don't care about political issues, and those who don't have the time to devote to politics. In 1980 and 1984, the use of pre- and postelection interviews made those in the sample especially aware of politics.

Table 2–1 compares the percentage in the CPS surveys who said they had voted in congressional races with the percentage of the public that actually voted in congressional races from 1978 through 1984. On the average, 58% of those interviewed reported that they voted. During the same years, about 42% of the American public actually did vote.

Some of the difference between the two figures can be accounted for by "overreporting." A CPS voter validation check against actual 1980 voting records indicates that about 5% of the people in the surveys claim to have voted in congressional races when they have not. Still, the actual voting turnout in the sample is probably about 53%, about 11% higher than for the population as a whole. That difference suggests substantially greater political activity among those surveyed than among citizens in general.

Not only does the composition of the samples tend to overrepresent the politically active and interested, so does the interview process. Just as some respondents say they voted when they did not, some will say they knew how the incumbent voted when they did not. For example, when asked to place themselves or a candidate on a scale measuring support for more defense spending, some will make some kind of middling placement before they will admit to not having thought much about the issue. Thus, sampling and interviewing tend to bias the research so as to exaggerate citizen knowledge.

In addition to bias in sampling and interviewing, bias will enter the analysis in the choice of measures for different properties (for example, in the choice of questions used to measure citizen knowledge). In deference to the general acceptance of the assumptions under test, such choices will always be made so as to bias the result in favor of showing

TABLE 2–1 Reported Turnout for Congressional Races among CPS Respondents and Actual Nationwide Turnout

	Reported CPS	Actual Nationwide
1978	48%	35%
1980	65%	47%
1982	54%	38%
1984	65%	48%
Average	58%	42%

Source: CPS studies and the *Statistical Abstract of the United States, 1986.*

that the assumptions are supported and that policy distance from the constituent does make a difference in whether a representative is reelected.

METHODOLOGICAL APPROACH

The analysis proceeds in four steps. First, an estimate of citizen knowledge of incumbent House members and of the policies they have supported is made. Second, an investigation is made of the willingness of knowledgeable citizens to reward and punish on the basis of policy differences between themselves and the incumbent. This includes an estimate of what might be called the "provocation threshold," the extent and direction of deviation by the representative necessary to provoke electoral retaliation by voters. Third, based on the provocation threshold and the likely distribution of policy positions in a district, an estimate is made of the support an incumbent is likely to garner by adopting different ideological positions. And fourth, based on 1980 election results, an estimate is made of the probability that policy deviation is decisive in a reelection race.

Estimates of knowledge and willingness to punish are made both for citizens in general and for voters. Previous studies that focused exclusively on citizens in general tended to show that constituents don't know enough to be able to reward and punish policy deviation by their representatives (see, especially, Hurley and Hill [1980]). Previous studies that focused exclusively on voters are more divided in their findings, but most showed some association between policy distance from the incumbent and vote choice (see, especially, Wright [1978], Johannes and McAdams [1980], and Wright and Berkman [1986]). It may be that voters are substantially more knowledgeable than citizens in general. By investigating both constituency and voter samples, it is possible to determine whether that is the case. If it proves so, only voters, among all constituents, may behave as the myth of constituency control would suggest. If members are responsive to potential electoral rewards and punishment, they may be responsive only to the voters and not to the constituency as a whole.

A number of previous studies have investigated one or more of the properties measured here. Stokes and Miller (1962) and Mann and Wolfinger (1980) investigated the extent to which constituents recognize their representatives. Hurley and Hill (1980) investigated the extent to which constituents could correctly identify the policy positions supported by their representatives. Weissberg (1976), Wright (1978), Abramowitz (1980), Johannes and McAdams (1981), and Wright and Berkman (1986) all looked at the association between policy distance from the representative and vote choice. Wright (1978), Abramowitz (1980), Johannes and McAdams (1981), and Wright and Berkman (1986) presented equations showing the effect of one or another measure of policy distance on vote choice. However, no analysis of individual voters has attempted to quantify the aggregate effects of policy distance on reelection prospects.

KNOWLEDGE

Recognizing the Incumbent

As argued in the last chapter, in order for citizens to reward and punish representatives, they must at least be able to distinguish representatives from nonrepresentatives on election day. It is not necessary for people to have memorized the incumbent's name—they need only be able to recognize the incumbent by either name or party, given both pieces of information (since this information would be on the ballot).

In the CPS surveys the interviewers gave the respondents the names and parties of the major-party nominees for the House. After several questions on feelings about the candidates, they asked, "Do you happen to know if either of these candidates, [names of the candidates], was already in the U.S. House of Representatives before the election?" (In single-candidate districts, the question was modified to ask if they happened to know if the candidate was already in the House.)

Table 2–2 shows the percentage of constituents who could correctly recognize the name or party of the incumbent. Those constituents are classified as able to recognize the incumbent.[1]

As Table 2–2 shows, the percentage who could correctly recognize their representative was quite steady from 1978-1984, about 66% of those interviewed. Thus, only about 66 out of every 100 *constituents* had the minimum knowledge to judge incumbents' policies.

The percentage among *voters*, however, was much higher. Of the 601 who voted in the 1980 election (when there was a check to determine who did vote), 580, or 97%, could recognize the incumbent. Knowledge was sufficiently widespread among the voters for them to behave as the myth would suggest.

TABLE 2–2   Percentage Who Can Recognize the Incumbent by Name or Party

	Percentage	(N)
1978	64%	(2029)
1980	69%	(1310)
1982	65%	(1229)
1984	65%	(1860)

Source: CPS Studies.

Knowing the Incumbent's Policy Positions

For a person to support or oppose a reelection bid on the basis of policy differences, recognition of the incumbent is not enough; it is also necessary that the person have *at least some* knowledge of the incumbent's policy positions.

Strict (Issue-by-Issue) Control. There are a number of ways to measure knowledge of the incumbent's policy positions. A strict interpretation of the myth of constituency control would suggest that the representative should fear citizen retaliation every time he or she has to cast a vote. Such an interpretation would also suggest that citizens should know how their representatives voted on every bill. Citizen knowledge, under that strict interpretation, would be measured by the percentage of people who could name *every* position taken by the incumbent. Obviously, the percentage who could do so would be negligible, so there is no sense in attempting such a measurement.

Approaching the measurement problem from the opposite end of the spectrum, one could find the percentage who cannot remember their representative's position on *any* bill. If they cannot recall even a single vote, they would certainly have difficulty rewarding or punishing the representative for his or her voting.

In the 1978 survey, the only survey to examine the question, respondents were asked, "Was there any bill in particular that you remember how [name of the incumbent] voted on in the last couple of years?" Only 14% (183/1300) of those who could recognize the incumbent could remember his or her vote on even a single bill.

Since only 64% of the constituents could recognize their representatives in 1978, that meant that just 9% (14% of 64%) of all constituents could both recognize their representative and his or her position on any particular bill. Assuming that the 1978 figure is representative, the highest percentage of constituents that might reward or punish a member of Congress for a vote on any specific bill is 9%. And even that figure assumes that there is some specific bill that all 9% are recalling.

It should be remembered that this poor recall occurs immediately after a campaign in which the incumbent's voting might have been an issue. Furthermore, the 9% figure makes no allowance for people who might be mistaken in their recall, or who might have said they remembered a vote when they had nothing clearly in mind.

Clearly, only a handful of citizens (if any) can exercise control in the strict sense of watching particular positions the representative takes and rewarding or punishing on the basis of those positions.

Loose (General Ideological) Control. If citizen control is exercised by most citizens, it must be control in a looser sense: control not over specific votes, but over general positions. Citizens might reward and punish their representatives based on knowledge of their general voting records, even though they do not know votes on specific issues.[2] If that were the case, of course, citizen control would not be complete. A member of Congress might "get away with" occasional votes that would not meet with constituency approval so long as he or she generally voted the way the constituents wanted.

Even this looser type of control requires some general knowledge of the representative's policy positions. The percentage of constituents and voters with the requisite general knowledge can be estimated by the percentage who can correctly evaluate how liberal or conservative their representatives are.

The CPS surveys ask respondents to place their representatives on seven-point issue scales. One of those scales is an ideology scale on which representatives may be placed anywhere from "extremely liberal" to "extremely conservative." Correct placement of the incumbent on that ideology scale is the criterion adopted here for classifying a constituent as knowing the incumbent's policy position. To make the comparison between constituents and voters as direct as possible, the check on correctness of position was made for the year (1980) in which there were data on voters (that also happens to be the year in which recognition of incumbents was most widespread).[3]

Placement of the representative on the ideology scale can be determined directly from CPS data. The correctness of that placement has to be determined by comparison with the voting record of the incumbent. The correctness of placement for respondents is determined by comparing each respondent's perception of where the incumbent stood with standard ratings of that incumbent's liberalism (his or her Americans for Democratic Action [ADA] rating) or conservatism (his or her Americans for Constitutional Action [ACA] rating) for 1979 and 1980. Both the ADA and ACA ratings go from 0 to 100. To be as generous as possible in evaluating respondents as knowledgeable, the placement of the incumbent by the respondent was coded as correct if the respondent's placement matched *either* the ADA or ACA rating shown in the chart below in 1979 *or* 1980:

Respondent's Placement of Incumbent	ADA Score *or* (ACA) Score of Incumbent in Either 1979 or 1980	
Extremely Liberal	70+	(0-30)
Liberal	51+	(0-49)
Slightly Liberal	51-80	(20-49)
Moderate	25-75	(25-75)
Slightly Conservative	20-49	(51-80)
Conservative	0-49	(51+)
Extremely Conservative	0-30	(70+)

TABLE 2–3   **Percentage of Constituents and Voters Correctly Placing the Ideology of the Incumbent, 1980**

	Constituents	Voters
Number in Sample	1310	601
Number Recognizing Incumbent	903	580
Number Placing Incumbent	570	401
Number Correctly Placing Incumbent	416	295
Percent Correctly Placing Incumbent	32%	49%

Source: 1980 CPS Study.

Given the wide range of allowable scores for each category and the fact that the incumbent could fall in that range for either of two rating organizations in either of the two years, this measure should not under-estimate the percentage knowing their representative's position.

Table 2–3 shows the percentage of all constituents and all voters who could both recognize their representative and correctly place that representative on the ideology scale.[4]

A generous estimate is that just under one third of the constituents and one half of the voters have the minimum knowledge that is a prerequisite for judging incumbents' policies. They know who their incumbent is and roughly what his or her policies have been.[5]

JUDGING INCUMBENTS' POLICIES

Even though they are not a majority of all voters, if everyone with the minimum knowledge rewarded and punished incumbents on the basis of policy positions, they would be numerous enough to determine a substantial percentage of reelection races. However, not everyone with the requisite knowledge votes on the basis of policy distance from the incumbent. People may cast their votes for any number of other reasons, ranging from how honest to how photogenic the incumbent is. Deference to the incumbent, party loyalty, personal loyalty, or lack of an attractive alternative may lead people to vote to reelect regardless of how distant the representative's policies are from their own.[6]

Furthermore, not every deviation by the representative will provoke voter retaliation, even from those who do judge incumbents' policy deviation. It seems likely that some, maybe nearly all, voters judge whether a particular deviation should be punished by *comparing the observed deviation to the deviation that would have been expected from any alternative representative.*[7] For those voters, the extent and direction of incumbents' deviations will be critical in determining whether to mete out punishment.

Small deviations will not be punished by voters who deem it likely that any other representative would also have deviated by a small amount from the most-desirable ideological position. Deviations by Republican incumbents to the left of voters' preferences will not be punished by voters who think it likely that a Democratic incumbent would have been even further left. Deviation by Democratic incumbents to the right of voters' preferences will similarly be tolerated by those thinking that a Republican incumbent would probably have been even further right. Only if incumbents' deviations cross a provocation threshold will they trigger punishment at the voting booth.

The Reasons People Give
for Liking and Disliking Incumbents

Looking at the reasons people give for liking and disliking incumbents is a very rough measure of the extent to which people are making judgments on the basis of policy differences. The questions asked by the Michigan researchers are open-ended, leading to validity and reliability problems in coding responses. Many people are unwilling or unable to tell why they like or dislike the incumbent, and there is no guarantee that the reasons for their judgments are the same as the reasons given by those who do respond to the researchers' questions. Furthermore, many would argue that some who vote on the basis of policy distance are unable to articulate their reasoning when asked likes and dislikes; hence, any method that relies on articulated reasons would understate willingness to reward and punish (Erikson, 1971; Wright, 1978; Gant and Davis, 1984).

Nevertheless, looking at the reasons people cite for liking and disliking incumbents is the only way to get even a rough estimate of the percentage of all *constituents* who are basing judgments on policy distance. Following this analysis of the reasons constituents give is an analysis of the votes cast in 1980 to verify existence of a provocation threshold and to delineate its boundaries.

People offer many different reasons for liking or disliking candidates. While some like or dislike candidates' voting records, others base their preferences on anything from physical appearance to perception of honesty. Many vote traditional party lines regardless of who the candidate is.

Two questions regarding likes and dislikes are used in the 1980 and 1982 CPS surveys:

"Is there anything in particular that you liked about [name of candidate]?"
"Is there anything in particular that you did not like about [name of candidate]?"

Respondents are asked to list up to four things that they liked and disliked about both the Democratic and Republican candidates. The responses to those questions are coded into hundreds of categories by the Michigan researchers. Table 2–4 shows the percentage of responses falling into categories that might show some concern over policy positions the incumbent had taken.

The year-to-year results are quite consistent. Only 2-3% of the reasons given deal directly with the candidates' voting records or records of public service (CPS coding places both reasons in a single category). Respondents were more likely to say they liked a candidate's speaking ability than they were to say they liked his or her voting record.

A total of 39% of the reasons given could, by some stretch of the imagination, have been reactions to incumbents' policy stances. (Here are included reasons such as "kept campaign promises," "helped the district's economy," "supports Republican policies," "anti far right," "pro lower taxes," and "pro labor.")

Apparently even citizens with the requisite knowledge are more likely to judge incumbents on the basis of other criteria than on the basis of their policy stances. Still, knowledgeable voters show some concern regarding incumbents' policies, and that concern might be a primary determinant of voting in races where the incumbents are seen as deviating substantially from the preferred positions of the voters.

TABLE 2–4   Reasons Given for Liking and Disliking Candidates: 1980 and 1982[8]

1980		
Number of Reasons Given	1858	
Number (%) of Reasons Citing Voting Record or Record of Public Service	56	(3%)
Number (%) of Reasons Citing Type of Job Done, How Well (S)He Represents District, or How Well (S)He Kept Campaign Promises	309	(17%)
Number (%) of Reasons Citing Any Policy or Policies or Support for Any Group	362	(19%)
1982		
Number of Reasons Given	2058	
Number (%) of Reasons Citing Voting Record or Record of Public Service	48	(2%)
Number (%) of Reasons Citing Type of Job Done, How Well (S)He Represents District, or How Well (S)He Kept Campaign Promises	299	(15%)
Number (%) of Reasons Citing Any Policy or Policies or Support for Any Group	462	(22%)

Source: 1980 and 1982 CPS Studies.

How People Vote

It is possible to use CPS data to determine the pattern of association, if any, between policy distance from the incumbent and likelihood of voting for that incumbent.

Policy Distance. The policy distance between what the individual favors and what the incumbent has supported is best measured by what the individual perceives that distance to be. It is perceived distance, even if that is not the actual distance, that will motivate behavior.[9]

The perceived policy distance between each person and his or her representative is measured by the difference between what the person reports as his or her score on the seven-point ideology scale and what the person reports as the representative's score on that same scale. Thus, respondents who see the incumbent as having the same ideological position as themselves have a score of 0. Respondents who see the incumbent as one scale step away have a score of + or − 1, the sign indicating whether the incumbent is to the right or left of the respondent, and so on.

Likelihood of Voting for the Incumbent. Each respondent is evaluating his or her distance from a specific representative. Whether the respondent voted for or against that representative is known, but whether the respondent would have voted differently if the perceived distance from the representative had been different cannot be known. What can be compared is the voting behavior of those groups of respondents who were varying distances from their representatives. Those comparisons can verify (1) whether policy distance tends to be negatively associated with support, (2) whether there are some voters who clearly do not judge incumbents on the basis of policy distance, (3) whether there are sharp increases in likelihood of voting against the incumbent (provocation thresholds) associated with specific policy distances, and (4) if the thresholds exist, whether they are at similar absolute distances but in different directions for incumbents of different parties.

Findings. Table 2–5 reports the percentages of those with the requisite knowledge who voted for and against reelection by their perceived policy distance from the incumbent.

Table 2–5 gives evidence that policy distance has an impact on voting, but it is far from the sole determinant of voting, even for these knowledgeable voters. There is a generally negative association between distance and support, but 6-13% of the voters fail to reward incumbents who support the policies they want the most, and 25-27% do reward incumbents who are three or more steps (about half a spectrum) away from what they want.

There is also evidence of provocation thresholds. First, small devia-

TABLE 2–5   Perceived Policy Distance of Incumbent and Vote Choice, by Party of the Incumbent

Republican Incumbents

	Policy Distance of Incumbent					
	2 Steps To Left	1 Step To Left	Zero	1 Step To Right	2 Steps To Right	3+ Steps To Right
Voted For Reelection	75%	82%	94%	84%	57%	27%
Voted Against Reelection	25%	18%	6%	16%	43%	73%
(N)	(4)	(22)	(34)	(19)	(7)	(11)

Democratic Incumbents

	Policy Distance of Incumbent					
	3+ Steps To Left	2 Steps To Left	1 Step To Left	Zero	1 Step To Right	2 Steps To Right
Voted For Reelection	25%	38%	83%	87%	92%	83%
Voted Against Reelection	75%	62%	17%	13%	8%	17%
(N)	(28)	(21)	(41)	(46)	(13)	(6)

(Tables based only on races with major-party competition)

Source: 1980 CPS Study.

tions are not punished, regardless of the incumbent's party. Incumbents one step to the left or right of the voter are supported to virtually the same extent as are incumbents with the same ideology as the voter. Second, greater deviations also go largely unpunished if they are in the direction typical of the opposition party. Only 25% were willing to punish Republicans two or more steps to the left of their preferred position; only 17% were willing to punish Democrats two or more steps to the right of that preference. However, knowledgeable voters were willing to deal out punishment to Republicans who were two, three, or more steps to the right of their preferred position, and to Democrats who were similar distances to the left. In the nonprovocative range (from far to the left to one step to the right for Republican incumbents; from far to the right to one step to the left for Democratic incumbents) an average of 86-87% of the voters supported the incumbent. Once the provocation threshold was crossed, support dropped substantially, with 43-75% voting to replace the incumbent.

THE EFFECT OF IDEOLOGICAL POSITIONING

No ideological position adopted by the incumbent is likely to gain or lose the ballots of all those voting on the basis of policy distance. Any position the incumbent could adopt would be close enough to some of those judging policies to gain their votes, even if it were far enough away from others to lose theirs. In general, incumbents have a great deal of leeway in the positions they adopt without having to fear electoral retaliation. They are first protected by the wide nonprovocative range for each voter and the high level of support given the incumbents who are perceived to be within that nonprovocative range. When perceived to be beyond the provocation threshold, they are still protected by the failure of a large minority to punish them for that deviation.

For any position an incumbent might have adopted, it is possible to calculate the support that he or she would probably have gotten among the knowledgeable voters. That calculation is based on the support evidenced by groups at varying distances from the incumbent's position (given in Table 2–5) once an estimate has been made of ideological distribution of the knowledgeable voters in that incumbent's constituency. For 1980, the distribution of ideologies in an incumbent's constituency can be estimated from the national distribution of ideologies for constituents of Republican and Democratic incumbents with specific perceived ideologies. Table 2–6 displays two of those distributions using the CPS seven-point scale.

As can be seen from the distributions, 1980 was a year in which voters leaned toward the conservative end of the spectrum, especially in districts represented by conservative or extremely conservative Republican incumbents. That conservatism protected Republican incumbents, even if they were perceived as extremely conservative by their constituents. An extremely conservative incumbent would have been within the nonprovocative range of only conservative and extremely conservative constituents, but they included 50% of all the knowledgeable voters in the Republican's district. Since knowledgeable voters rewarded Republican incumbents in their nonprovocative range with 87% of their votes (see Table 2–5), an extremely conservative Republican incumbent could expect to get 87% of the ballots from that half of the voters. An extremely conservative Republican could also expect to get 57% of the vote from those two steps to his or her left—the 20.5% of the voters who considered themselves slightly conservative. Finally, the extremely conservative Republican could expect 27% of the votes from the rest of the knowledgeable voters, those three or more steps to the incumbent's left. Overall, an extremely conservative Republican could expect to get $(.87 \times 50\%) + (.57 \times 20.5\%) + (.27 \times 29.5\%)$, or 63.2% of the votes from the group

TABLE 2-6   Ideological Distributions for Constituents of Republican Incumbents Perceived As Conservative or Extremely Conservative and Democratic Incumbents Perceived as Liberal or Extremely Liberal

CONSTITUENTS OF REPUBLICAN INCUMBENTS (N=44)

Extremely Liberal	Liberal	Slightly Liberal	Moderate	Slightly Conserv.	Conservative	Extremely Conserv.
2.2%	2.2%	15.9%	9.1%	20.5%	40.9%	9.1%

CONSTITUENTS OF DEMOCRATIC INCUMBENTS (N=42)

Extremely Liberal	Liberal	Slightly Liberal	Moderate	Slightly Conserv.	Conservative	Extremely Conserv.
9.5%	19.0%	9.5%	21.4%	11.9%	28.6%	0%

Source: 1980 CPS Study.

of knowledgeable voters in the district. And that was the lowest level of support any Republican incumbent could expect to get from the knowledgeable voters on the basis of the policy positions he or she had adopted while in office! Any Republican perceived as less than extremely conservative would have picked up even more votes from the knowledgeable voters, as more knowledgeable voters would have been within the nonprovocative range. No Republican incumbent who lost in 1980 could blame the defeat on the ideological positions he or she had supported.

That does not mean that voters did not punish any policy deviation in 1980. Similar calculations for Democratic incumbents show that being perceived as an extreme liberal probably cost a Democratic incumbent in a typical district the majority among the group of knowledgeable voters. Because the voters tilted slightly to the right even in the typical district represented by a liberal or extremely liberal Democrat in 1980, an incumbent perceived as an extreme liberal could expect to get support from only 43.6% of the knowledgeable voters. (A Democratic incumbent perceived as a liberal could expect to get support from 51% of those voters.)

Ideological positioning may then have been critical for some Democratic incumbents in 1980. Losing the majority among the knowledgeable voters, roughly 49% of all voters, did not necessarily cost even extreme liberals their seats. However, if the extreme liberal got only 43.6% of the ballots among that 49% of voters, he or she needed over 56% of the ballots from the less-knowledgeable votes to win reelection. An extreme liberal who lost with better than 46.7% of the vote probably did score a majority among the less knowledgeable, but lost because of voter retaliation against the extremism of his or her ideology.

THE DECISIVENESS OF POLICY POSITIONING

The policy positions that an incumbent has taken can be decisive in two ways: the positions may have cost enough support among knowledgeable voters to lose an election that would otherwise have been won, or the positions may have gained enough support among knowledgeable voters to win an election that would otherwise have been lost.

Losing Elections That Might Have Been Won

As the calculations above indicated, policy deviation could not have been decisive in the first sense in 1980 for any but those Democratic incumbents perceived as extreme liberals. All Republican incumbents and all Democratic incumbents except the extreme liberals probably won a majority among the knowledgeable voters. If they lost the election, it was because of factors other than policy deviation.

Policy deviation may have led to defeat for those perceived as extremely liberal Democrats. As calculated above, extremely liberal Democrats who lost with over 46.7% of the vote might reasonably attribute their losses to the policy positions they adopted. Policy positions were probably not decisive for extreme liberals who got less than 46.7% of the vote, as they probably would have lost even if they had shifted far enough to the right to get majority support among the knowledgeable voters.

Table 2–7 lists the Democratic incumbents whose ideologies might have been decisive in losing races. The list includes those who lost with more than 46.7% of the vote who could have been correctly perceived as extremely liberal by the definition used earlier in this chapter (ACA scores of less than 30 or ADA of more than 70 for 1979 or 1980).

It is extremely unlikely that the incumbents' ideological positions were, in fact, decisive in all eleven of these losing efforts. It is most unlikely that *all* of these incumbents were perceived as extremely liberal by *all* of their constituents (only 5% of all respondents with Democratic incumbents saw their representatives as extremely liberal). To the extent that voters saw these representatives as liberal rather than extremely liberal, the representatives got a higher percentage of the vote among the knowledgeable voters than was calculated above; thus, ideology probably was not decisive for those listed in Table 2–7 as losing by margins as wide as 53% to 47%.

Furthermore, if these candidates were perceived as extreme liberals, the distribution of ideologies among the knowledgeable voters

TABLE 2–7   Incumbents Whose Ideologies Might Have Cost Them Reelection

Incumbent	Percent of Vote	ACA Rating*
James Corman (D-CA 21)	48	7
Lionel Van Deerlin (D-CA 42)	47	6
Bob Carr (D-MI 6)	49	26
Andrew Maguire (D-NJ 7)	47	14
Lester Wolff (D-NY 6)	47	26
Al Ullman (D-OR 2)	47	19
Peter Kostmayer (D-PA 8)	49	24
Bob Eckhardt (D-TX 8)	48	2
Herbert Harris (D-VA 8)	49	11
Joseph Fisher (D-VA 10)	49	21
Alvin Baldus (D-WI 3)	49	7

(*Rating is 1979-1980 average)

Sources: Barone and Ujifusa 1982; Congressional Quarterly, 1981.

in these districts may well have been shifted further left than the distribution that was assumed in the calculations above. Because there were so few respondents who saw their representatives as extreme liberals, the distribution used to calculate expected percentage among knowledgeable voters was the distribution in districts represented by liberal as well as very liberal representatives. If these incumbents were almost universally viewed as extremely liberal, they probably represented districts with a slightly more liberal group of knowledgeable voters. If that were the case, the group would have given the incumbent a somewhat higher percentage of the vote than was calculated above. Hence, those listed as losing by a wider margin in Table 2–7 probably did not lose because of their ideologies.

The list in Table 2–7, therefore, probably exaggerates the number of races in which the ideological position of the incumbent might have been decisive in losing a race in 1980. Eleven is the maximum number of races in which constituents punished representatives for policy deviation; the actual number is probably substantially smaller.

Winning Races That Might Have Been Lost

Ideological positioning might also have been decisive for incumbents who avoided extreme ideological positions but still won narrowly. Adoption of more extreme positions might have cost them enough support among the knowledgeable voters to have lost the election.

Table 2–8 lists all of the incumbents who had less than a 20% vote margin over their opponents and who did not adopt positions that knowledgeable voters could have seen as extremely liberal for Democratic incumbents or extremely conservative for Republican incumbents.[10] The position adopted by the incumbent was unlikely to have been decisive in races won by 20% or more. Positioning could also not be decisive in races won by extremely liberal Democrats or extremely conservative Republicans: had they adopted any other positions, they would have won by even more. The list in Table 2–8 is quite short as the winning margins in House races tend to be very large, while the number of Democrats who adopted positions that could not be seen as extremely liberal and the number of Republicans who adopted positions that could not be seen as extremely conservative tend to be quite small.

A reasonable case can be made that the ideological positions adopted by the first nine incumbents listed in Table 2–8 were decisive in their victories. Had those Democrats adopted positions that could have been seen as extremely liberal or had those Republicans adopted positions that could have been seen as extremely conservative, they probably would have provoked sufficient retaliation among the knowledgeable voters to have lost.

It is unlikely that positioning was decisive in the last four races on

TABLE 2–8   Incumbents Who Won Relatively Close Races—Excluding Those Iden-
tifiable As Extremely Liberal Democrats or Extremely Conservative
Republicans

Incumbent	Percent of Vote	ACA Rating*
David Evan (D-IN 6)	50	61
Andrew Jacobs (D-IN 11)	57	62
Carl Pursell (R-MI 2)	57	37
William Green (R-NY 18)	57	37
Ike Andrews (D-NC 4)	53	37
Stephen Neal (D-NC 5)	51	54
Marc Marks (R-PA 24)	50	45
Jim Mattox (D-TX 5)	51	42
Jack Hightower (D-TX 13)	55	52
Dan Mica (D-FL 11)	59	42
W. G. Hefner (D-NC 8)	59	36
Thomas Luken (D-OH 2)	59	38
James Jones (D-OK 1)	58	40

(*Rating is 1979-1980 average)

Source: Barone and Ujifusa, 1982.

the list, as those candidates had fairly large margins of victory and were probably seen as liberals in their districts. Had they been seen as extreme liberals instead, their support among the knowledgeable voters would have dropped (as estimated above, from 51% to 43.6%), but that drop would not have been enough to have cost them the election.

Summary

Analyses of the narrow wins and losses show a maximum of 20, but probably fewer, races in which the ideological position of the incumbent was probably decisive. There were 389 reelection races in 1980, so ideological positioning was probably decisive in 5% or fewer of the races.[11] However, *1980 was a year in which many incumbents either lost or won by narrow margins*. If a similar analysis were done for 1986, when 98% of incumbents won their reelection races, ideological positioning would prove to be decisive in far less than 5% of the races.

REVIEWING THE EVIDENCE REGARDING CITIZEN BEHAVIOR

This chapter has looked at survey data to see if there is evidence that citizens behave as the myth of constituency control suggests they do. In particular, evidence for assumptions regarding citizen knowledge and willingness to reward and punish incumbents based on policy distance from those incumbents was investigated. The evidence is not strongly supportive of the myth.

There apparently are citizens who know their representatives and judge them on the basis of policy distance. Furthermore, that judgment of policy distance is apparently a complex process in which perceived distance from the incumbent is measured relative to the distance that would have been expected from a representative of the opposing party.

However, those who are able and willing to vote on the basis of policy distance are a small minority of the whole constituency. Less than one third of all constituents and one half of all voters have the knowledge needed to judge incumbents on the basis of policy distance. Of those with the requisite knowledge, only 39% list policy positions taken by the incumbent among the things they like or dislike about their representative. Given the wide margins by which most reelection races are decided and the diversity of ideological preferences within a constituency, the minority of knowledgeable, policy-evaluative constituents are rarely decisive in a reelection race.

The evidence is that most citizens cannot exercise control over their representatives, and that those who can often refrain from doing so. Only a minority of voters, and an even smaller minority of constituents, behave as the assumptions underlying the myth of constituency control would suggest.

In defense of the myth, it is likely that the assumptions would be better supported if data were available on citizen knowledge of and voting response to Senate incumbents, rather than House incumbents. A significantly higher percentage of constituents, though not of voters, can recognize the Senate incumbent than can recognize the House incumbent. The probability of reelection of Senate incumbents is lower than that of House incumbents, which suggests that the same responsiveness to policy distance by the voters is probably more decisive in Senate races than in House races.

Weighing against those factors is the six-year term for senators. Constituents cannot exercise control over senators for many years after they are elected. Whatever the evidence on constituent response to senators would have been, a valid study of that response is not now possible as the Center for Political Studies interviews many fewer people regarding Senate races than House races, and those they do interview are not representative of the states in which they reside.

Also in defense of the myth, it is possible that more citizens behave in accordance with its underlying assumptions, but researchers are unable to find evidence of that behavior. Citizens may have knowledge that they could not or would not display. Citizens may have voted on the basis of policy concerns, but were unable to remember or articulate their reasoning or the policy distance that they felt separated them from their representative (Erickson, 1971; Wright, 1978; Gant and Davis, 1984).

However, every effort has been made to overstate support for the assumptions. The *evidence* is that relatively few citizens are able and willing to hold incumbents accountable for the policies that they have supported.

ENSURING RESPONSIVE REPRESENTATION

Because even knowledgeable voters will tolerate a range of ideological positions and will strongly support incumbents so long as they are within that range, the ideological positions adopted by incumbents are probably decisive in no more than 5% of the reelection races. It is hard, therefore, to have much confidence in the argument that elections ensure the responsiveness of representatives to their constituents.

There may be a *single issue* that is so critical to a district that responsiveness on that issue can be assured. Negative campaigning in recent years may have raised voter knowledge of policy positions and increased voting on the basis of that knowledge in specific districts. The *fear* that his or her race might be one of the few determined by the policy distance from constituents might produce responsiveness in a representative, even if the voters do not compel responsiveness. However, the evidence at the level of the individual voter does not support the argument that elections generally *ensure* or *compel* ideological responsiveness by the representative to his or her constituents.

Furthermore, if the possibility of rewards or punishment at the polls is sufficient to encourage responsiveness, it is unlikely that the responsiveness will be to the constituency as a whole. Only voters can dangle rewards and threaten punishment. If elections encourage responsiveness, they encourage responsiveness to voters—especially politically-knowledgeable, policy-evaluative voters—not to the constituency as a whole. If the voters hold policy positions that are representative of the policy positions held by the constituency as a whole, then the reward of victory and fear of defeat will encourage responsiveness to the constituency as a whole. However, considerable research suggests that voters, especially politically-knowledgeable, policy-evaluative voters, are not representative of the constituency as a whole. Their socioeconomic class, hence their ideological preference (including their support for civil liberties), is likely to differ from that of the constituency as a whole. Consequently, any responsiveness encouraged by elections is likely to be responsiveness to an unrepresentative minority of the constituency.

NOTES

[1]Mann and Wolfinger (1980) report a higher percentage able to recognize incumbents, but they consider anyone who is willing to rate the incumbent on a feeling ther-

mometer as "recognizing the incumbent." That inflates the percentage classified as recognizing the incumbent in two ways: (1) some people may attempt to please the interviewer by giving a rating to any name given them, and (2) people may recognize and rate a name, but not recognize that the name is that of the incumbent member of Congress (for example, they may have heard of Bill Smith and even have generally warm feelings toward him without knowing that Bill is their representative). Since the surveys specifically ask whether respondents can recall if the candidates were in the House, there is no need to go to the feeling thermometers for an indirect measure of ability to recognize the incumbent. (The feeling thermometers are more appropriate for determining the name recognition of the incumbent—that is, whether people have heard of the incumbent, not whether they recognize him or her as the incumbent.)

[2]Most of those who have written on the subject expect no more than this looser type of control (see Miller and Stokes, 1963; Sullivan and O'Connor, 1972; Clausen, 1973; Fenno, 1977; Wright, 1978; Johannes and McAdams, 1981; Gant and Davis, 1984; Bond, Covington, and Fleisher, 1985).

[3]Scales other than the ideology scale could be used, but they would produce lower estimates of knowledgeable constituents than is obtained using the 1980 ideology scale. In general, a lower percentage of respondents places incumbents on the other issue scales than on the ideology scale, and respondents make more errors in placement on other issues than on ideology. Hurley and Hill (1980) found no other issue scale on which a majority of respondents could correctly place incumbents; for the ideology scale, 73% of the constituents could correctly place the incumbent. The wide range of scores taken as acceptable may account for the higher percentage correct. However, it is hard to call a person's evaluation incorrect if it accords with either the ACA or ADA ratings for either year.

[4]A few knowledgeable voters may have refused to answer this question, thus underestimating the percentage knowing the incumbent's position. However, a number who did not know the incumbent's position may have guessed it correctly, thus overestimating the percentage knowing the incumbent's position. While there is an attempt below to distinguish between correct and incorrect placement, there is no correction factor for those who may have guessed the correct placement.

[5]The estimate of constituent knowledge is a particularly generous one, as the percentage recognizing the incumbent (69%) was higher in 1980 than in any other year. Similarly, the percentage placing the incumbent on the ideology scale (63%) was higher in 1980 than in any other year.

[6]Deference is more widespread than one might think. For example, 30% of the respondents stated that if the representative was faced with a conflict between what the voters think is best and what he or she thinks is best, the representative should do what he or she thinks best. It seems that those people would be unlikely to reward and punish on the basis of policy deviation.

[7]There is no research prior to this that shows that voters make this comparison. However, that voters do make such a comparison is a reasonable synthesis and expansion of the theoretical and empirical work on spatial models and retrospective voting (Downs, 1957; Davis, Hinich, and Ordeshook, 1970; Bernstein, 1976; Fiorina, 1981; Wright and Berkman, 1986).

[8]The actual questions ask about the positions of the Democratic and Republican candidates. Candidates are restricted to just incumbents by controlling for type of congressional race. Total for code 217 is listed as number citing voting record or record of public service. Total for codes 222–225, 323, 324, and 327-332 is listed as number citing type of job done, how well (s)he represents district, or how well (s)he kept campaign promises. Total for codes 509-536, 605, 606, 801, 805-830, and 847-1297 is listed as number citing any policy or policies or support for any group.

[9]Abramowitz (1980) and Johannes and McAdams (1981) contrast the respondent's perception of his or her own position with the actual voting record of the incumbent, as evaluated by the Americans for Democratic Action (ADA). While that technique reduces reliance on perception, it has other disadvantages. Perhaps the most important is that it

assumes that the respondent and the ADA would classify the same positions as liberal, moderate, or conservative. That assumption is often going to be incorrect if the respondent bases his classification on a regional context.

[10]As previously defined, those would be Democrats who did not have ADA scores over 69 nor ACA scores under 30 and Republicans who did not have ADA scores under 30 nor ACA scores over 69 during 1979 or 1980.

[11]Excludes races in which the incumbent was convicted or indicted for a crime and races where the incumbent had served less than a full term.

THREE

Assumptions Regarding Constituencies

The myth of constituency control is built on the premise that deviation decreases the probability of reelection. As noted in Chapter 1, that premise can be stated as a hypothesis:

> Controlling for other variables, the more the policies voted for by the incumbent differ from those favored by his or her constituency, the lower the probability that the incumbent will get reelected.

This chapter tests the empirical support for that hypothesis. It then tests two bounded variants of the hypothesis based on the theory and findings presented in the last chapter regarding the comparative nature of the evaluation of incumbents' policy deviations. The chapter concludes with an estimate, for 1984, of the number of reelection races for the House in which the incumbent's ideology was decisive. This district-level analysis reinforces many of the results found at the constituent level.

PREVIOUS RESEARCH

Four studies have found at least suggestions of support for the hypothesis. In the pioneering study, Robert Erickson (1971) compared electoral support for conservative and liberal Republicans and for conservative and liberal Democrats. He did not directly test the hypothesis at issue here. However, his comparisons do bring evidence to bear on the hypothesis if one is willing to assume that, in general, conservative Republicans are likely to deviate further from their constituencies' wishes than are liberal Republicans, and liberal Democrats are likely to deviate further than are conservative Democrats.[1] Then, relatively small reelection margins for conservative Republicans and for liberal Democrats would be evidence that citizens are punishing representatives' deviations from the popular will.

Erikson found that in the 1950's and 1960's, conservative Democrats did *not* fare any better at the polls than did liberal Democrats. However, there was a suggestion of support for the hypothesis in his finding that conservative Republicans had a smaller margin of victory in House races than did more liberal Republicans.

The Erikson study was not intended as a direct test of the hypothesis and is, at best, seen as suggestive that a direct test of the hypothesis might be supportive. However, the study also casts doubts regarding the hypothesis as the margins for Democrats, who were in the majority, did not vary as the hypothesis would suggest. Furthermore, the late 1950's and the 1960's were poor years for conservative Republicans. In other years, Erikson might not have uncovered even the suggestion of support for the hypothesis that he found in the 1960's.

The first study that could be interpreted as a direct test of the hypothesis was a very limited investigation by Gerald Wright (1977) of the reelection attempts of those who had served on the House Judiciary Committee during the impeachment votes on President Richard Nixon. If one assumes that those who supported Nixon had deviated from what their constituencies wanted them to do, then the hypothesis would be supported by evidence that Nixon supporters ran worse than did those who opposed Nixon. A suggestion of support for the hypothesis can be seen in the finding that, after controlling for other variables, Republican supporters of Nixon ran 2% worse than did Republican opponents. However, that 2% difference among Republicans was not statistically significant, and support for Nixon had no effect at all on the reelection percentage of Democrats.

Somewhat more convincing support for the hypothesis was found by John Johannes and John McAdams (1981). They used the Americans for Democratic Action's (ADA's) evaluations of representatives' voting records as their measure of liberalism for each representative. As their measure of liberalism for each constituency, they used the percentage of the popular vote for George McGovern in 1972. Assuming that the degree of liberalism preferred by each district in its representative is a linear function of how liberal the constituency is, Johannes and McAdams measured the deviation of the representative from the preference of the constituency by the difference between the representative's liberalism and a linear transformation of the constituency's liberalism.[2]

While the Johannes and McAdams' measure of policy deviation was a substantial improvement over the measures used by Erikson and Wright, their overall analysis suffered because variables had to be measured at different points in time. Liberalism of the representative was measured for 1976; liberalism of the district was measured for 1972; and the reelection percentage of representatives was measured for 1978. Given the dramatic population changes in many districts, it is unclear that the 1972 vote was indicative of district liberalism in 1976. Even if it was, one cannot be sure that the extent of ideological discrepancy did not widen or narrow between 1976 and 1978.[3]

Johannes and McAdams' findings suggest some support for the hypothesis. There was a weak negative association between extent of deviation and reelection percentage. However, that association was not statistically significant when controlling for the percentage of the vote won by the representative in the previous election. More importantly, their equations (pp. 521-22) suggest that a deviation from median constituency preference of 33 points in ADA rating—a full one third of the entire spectrum—would cost an incumbent only about 6% of the vote. As the last chapter showed, House races are typically decided by such a large margin that the 6% is unlikely to deprive many candidates of reelection.

The most recent study suggesting some support for the hypothesis was by Kenny Whitby and Timothy Bledsoe (1986). Senators' ideological positions were measured by their Americans for Constitutional Action (ACA) ratings for three-year periods prior to a reelection race, the periods ranging from 1972-74 through 1982-84. The ideological preferences of constituencies were measured by two linear transformations (one per party) of the average vote for Reagan, 1980-84. Policy deviation was the difference between the ACA rating and the linear transformation of the Reagan vote for the senators' party.

In essence, Whitby and Bledsoe assumed that a given geographic constituency had different policy preferences for Republican and Democratic representatives. Those preferences might be thought of as the preferences of the Republican and Democratic constituencies within each state. Thus, their measures of policy deviation might be thought of as measuring the deviation of representatives from the preferences of their own party's constituency within the state.

Because there are so few senators running for reelection each year, Whitby and Bledsoe analyzed races over a series of elections. However, their measure of constituency preferences could only be obtained for 1980-84. This created very serious time-based validity problems. There is little reason to believe that constituency ideology was the same in 1972-74 as in 1980-84. A senator might have been in perfect agreement with his or her constituency in 1972-74, but that perfect agreement could not be noted by looking only at the constituency's preferences for 1980-84.

If one overlooks the validity problems with their measure, there is a suggestion of support in the Whitby and Bledsoe analysis. Specifically, they found support for the hypothesis for senators representing the 19 states with the most urban, well-educated populace.

Weak and ambiguous as the suggestions of support have been in these four studies, they are the strongest empirical evidence that has been uncovered to support the hypothesis. Evidence tending to contradict the hypothesis has been presented by Robert Weissberg (1981). In case studies of all 73 defeats of members of Congress running for reelection between 1968 and 1974, Weissberg was able to find only two instances where defeat could reasonably be traced back to policy deviation. Furthermore, substantial research on incumbents' "home styles" and the willingness of constituents to trust their representatives shows that many constituencies will not choose to punish trusted representatives for policy deviation (Fenno, 1978; Parker, 1987; Larson, 1987).

MEASUREMENT

Any test of the hypothesis involves measurement of (1) the extent of deviation of each representative's policies from the policies favored by his or her constituents and (2) the probability that the representative will get reelected. The first of those two variables is exceedingly difficult to measure in a way that all would consider valid.

Policy Deviation

The ideal measure of the extent of deviation of each representative's policies from the policies favored by his or her constituency would place both the constituency's preferences and the policies supported by the representative against the same kind of ruler and note the distance between them. Unfortunately, no such ruler exists. Instead one has to infer policy preferences for both constituencies and representatives from surveys or voting behavior. It is not possible to measure preferences very precisely, nor is it generally possible to use the same "ruler" for constituencies and representatives.

As no available measure of policy deviation is completely valid, the analyses in this chapter use three different measures:

(1) perceived constituency/representative differences on seven-point issue scales,
(2) differences between constituencies' opinions and representatives' voting, and
(3) constituency/representative voting differences.

Perceived constituency/representative differences. The first type of measure of policy deviation is based entirely upon aggregated responses to the CPS National Election Studies. In those surveys, respondents place both themselves and their representative on seven-point issue scales. The policy deviation of the representative from each constituent on each issue is measured by the absolute value of the difference between the respondent's position and the representative's perceived position. Thus, respondents who see the representative as having the same position as themselves have a score of 0. If the representative is seen as one scale step away, the score is 1, and so on. The measure of policy deviation of the representative from his or her constituency as a whole is the median of the deviations from individual constituents.[4]

This type of measure of policy deviation has some advantages. It uses basically the same "ruler" to measure the positions of the constituency and the representative. These measures can be made in different election years and can be applied to many issues each year.

There are, however, serious disadvantages to this type of measure. One is that it is based on what people perceive to be the representative's position. Because of the inaccuracy of respondents' perceptions, there is a question as to the validity of any perception-based measure (Wright, 1978).

An even more serious drawback to this kind of measure is the small number of districts that can be used and the small samples available to represent each district. Of all the CPS samples, only those in 1978 and 1980 were drawn to be representative of congressional districts. In those years respondents were interviewed in only about one fourth of the districts, and the number interviewed in each district was small. Districts had to be eliminated if no incumbent ran, if less than four respondents placed their representative on any issue scale, or if the race was apparently decided by some unusual scandal. That left 80 districts for analysis in 1978 and 53 districts for analysis in 1980; each district had an average of 10 respondents.[5]

There is considerable doubt regarding the validity of inferring constituency characteristics from such limited numbers of respondents in each district. Yet, Warren Miller and Donald Stokes (1962) presented a lengthy empirical justification for using samples almost this small to measure constituent opinion on issues, and their samples were not drawn to be representative of districts. In recent works, Partricia Hurley (1982), Donald McCrone and Walter Stone (1986), and Brad Lockerbie (1986) used these CPS samples to measure constituency opinion on the same issue scales as are used here.

If one could use only one measure of policy deviation, this would not be the measure of choice for most researchers. As one of three measures, it might disclose support for the hypothesis that would be hidden by other measures, measures at least partially based on voting behavior.

Constituencies' opinions and representatives' voting.   The second type of measure uses CPS surveys only to measure constituencies' positions on specific issues that had been voted on in Congress. For example, in 1978 respondents were asked, "Do you approve or disapprove of the proposed Equal Rights Amendment to the Constitution . . .?" Respondents were coded as being for or against. Based on the median opinion of the respondents, constituencies are then coded for, neutral, or against the ERA.

For this type of measure, representatives' positions are coded on the basis of how they voted on the issue in Congress. For example, on August 15, 1978, the House of Representatives voted on whether to allow states to rescind their ratifications of the Equal Rights Amendment. Representatives are coded as for, neutral, or against the ERA based on how they voted that day.

Policy deviation is measured by the difference between constituency opinion and congressional voting (basically following the procedure of Hurley and Hill, 1980; Hurley, 1982). In the ERA example, the policy deviation measure has three categories: representatives voted for the position their constituencies favored; they voted against the position their constituencies favored; or they adopted a position that was neither favored nor opposed by their constituents. This type of measure has more categories when there is either a wider range of opinion on the issue by the respondents or a series of votes on the issue by the representatives.

The major advantage of this type of measure, relative to the first type, is that it bases the representatives' positions on their behavior, not on the respondent's perception of that behavior. However, the second type of measure has a serious disadvantage relative to the first: The same "ruler" isn't used to measure both constituencies' and representatives' positions. The question asked of the respondent is not exactly the same as the one facing the member of Congress. For example, in measuring policy deviation on the ERA, respondents were asked if they favored the ERA, but the vote was on whether states should be allowed to rescind ratifications of the ERA. There is some chance that what is measured as policy deviation is partly a result of differences in wording between what is asked of the public and what is voted on by the representatives.

Again, this would not be the measure of choice for most researchers because of the small number of respondents used to determine constituency opinion. But, again, its use might disclose an association hidden by using other measures.

Constituency/representative voting differences.   The third type of measure infers constituency position on a liberal/conservative dimension from district voting in the 1984 presidential election. That election is used because it presents the clearest recent liberal/conservative confrontation in a year in which there was little Congressional reapportionment.

Constituency liberalism is measured by the percentage of the vote in each district going to Democratic candidate Walter Mondale. Those percentages are then converted to standardized scores (z-scores).

Representative liberalism is measured by (100-ACA rating).[6] Those ratings are also converted into standardized scores.

Using standardized scores ensures that all measures can be compared because they will all have the same average and same standard deviation. Policy deviation is simply measured by the absolute value of the difference between each constituency's standardized score and the standardized score of its representative. If the district and the representative are equally liberal, the policy deviation is 0. The farther apart they are, the higher the value of the deviation.

This type of measure is similar in some respects to the residual-based measure used by Johannes and McAdams. It has two major advantages over their measure: (1) all measures are taken for the same year—constituency liberalism for one year does not have to be compared with representative liberalism for another; and (2) constituency liberalism and representative liberalism are weighted equally in determining the final measure—a residual-based measure would weight representative liberalism more heavily than constituency liberalism.[7]

This third type of measure has the advantage, relative to the first two types of measures, of inferring constituency preference from the behavior of a large number of constituents rather than from the attitudes of a small number of respondents. An 80% vote for Mondale is a better indicator of district liberalism than is an average score of 6 out of 7 on a liberalism scale responded to by 10 individuals in that district.

Furthermore, by using this type of measure it is possible to compute policy deviation scores for virtually all members of Congress running for reelection.[8] That is not possible using CPS-based measures.

There are also disadvantages to using the third type of measure. First, it is possible to infer policy deviation only for the 1984 election. Second, constituency opinion is not available on specific issues, only on ideology in general. And third, the ideological measure is just an inference from voting on the 1984 presidential election. While that election did contrast candidates of markedly different ideologies, ideology was not the only basis for voting decisions.[9]

Furthermore, the standardized scores for constituencies and representatives are not based on the same measures. One standard deviation more liberal than the average Congressional district may not be the same degree of liberalism as is one standard deviation more liberal than the average representative.

If one had to rely on one measure of policy deviation, this would be it. It's not perfect, but it is better than the alternatives.

Fortunately, there is no need to rely on a single measure of policy deviation. All three types of measures are used in separate tests of the hypothesis. To the extent that analyses based on these markedly different types of measures point to the same conclusion regarding the hypothesis, confidence in that conclusion is greatly strengthened.

Probability of Reelection

Measuring the probability of reelection is a simpler task than measuring policy deviation. For races already run, the standard procedure is to estimate what *was* the probability of reelection from the actual election result. For example, one could estimate from the fact that an incumbent won an election that he or she had had a high probability of winning; from the fact that an incumbent lost an election, one could estimate that he or she had had a low probability of winning.

Using wins and losses to estimate probability of winning does not, however, work well for reelection races for the House. Losses by incumbents are too rare. The probability of losing a House race is so low that it is difficult to discern statistically significant differences in winning percentages regardless of any other differences among groups of representatives. If one discards from the sample those representatives involved in redistricting, sex scandals, or criminal activity, there are rarely more than 10-15 losers in the whole House of Representatives for any given year. If one tries to use winning and losing as the measure of probability of reelection, there simply is not enough variation in the dependent variable to be sure of what explains the little bit that does occur.

Instead of using wins and losses, it is standard to estimate what the probability of reelection was by the percentage of the vote received by the incumbent (in the general election and/or in the primary). Percentage of the vote is used as the dependent variable by Erikson (1971), Wright (1977), Johannes and McAdams (1981), and Whitby and Bledsoe (1986). It seems obvious that a representative who got 90% or 100% of the vote had a lower probablility of losing than did a representative who got 51%. Nevertheless, this type of measure has two serious weaknesses.

One, percentages above a certain number may not reflect real differences in the probability of getting reelected. Was a candidate who got 90% of the vote—or even 75% of the vote—really in more danger of losing than one who got 100%? Two, the difference between 49.9% and 50.1% of the vote is much more critical than the difference between 59.9% and 60.1%, both theoretically and practically; yet the relative importance of those differences will not be reflected when the dependent variable is percentage of the vote received.

Because this is the standard measure and because it is an interval variable, it is used despite its disadvantages, in the analyses where the independent variable is also interval. However, where the independent variable is ordinal, this variable is collapsed to form a measure distinguishing three categories of reelection results: losses, close wins (less than 60% of the vote), and easy wins. The ordinal measure does not exaggerate what may, especially in the upper category, be relatively small differences in reelection probability.

Control Variables

Party, seniority, and margin of victory in the previous race are all likely to affect the probability of reelection. It is quite possible that they also affect the extent of deviation of representatives from their constituencies. All three variables, therefore, are controlled in each of the analyses.

For much the same reasons, in analyses of voting in presidential election years, when the dependent variable is not calculated from the standardized vote for president there is also a control for the percentage of the presidential vote going to the more liberal or conservative presidential candidate (as an index of district liberalism).

When the independent and dependent variables are treated as ordinal, controls are done category by category, so there is no chance that influence of the independent variable will be obscured by covariance with a control variable or conditional effects of any type. A comparison of the bivariate and partial correlations for the interval-level analysis shows that the control variables are not obscuring the relationship there, either.

TESTING THE HYPOTHESIS

A series of analyses follow, each relating the various types of measures of policy deviation to the probability of reelection. The analyses are independent tests of the hypothesis.

Perceived Distance from Constituency and Probability of Reelection

Perceived distance of the constituency from the incumbent is measured by seven-point CPS scales for six issue areas for 1978: liberal/conservative ideology, government-guaranteed jobs, government aid to minorities, government medical insurance, women's equality, and rights of the accused. Previous research suggests that perceived distance along a liberal/conservative dimension is more likely to affect the voting of constituents than is the perceived distance on any single issue (Wright, 1978; Johannes and McAdams, 1981). Therefore, the analysis starts with the relationship between perceived ideological distance from the constituency and reelection result.

The zero del_1 for Table 3–1 indicates that the association between perceived distance and reelection is no stronger than would be expected by chance if distance from the constituency had no effect at all on reelection prospects.[10] While the two representatives who lost were not

TABLE 3–1   Perceived Ideological Distance from the Constituency and Reelection Result: 1978

		PERCEIVED DISTANCE FROM CONSTITUENCY*		
		Close	Moderate	Far
Reelection Result**	EasyWin	69%	82%	75%
	Close Win	31%	16%	17%
	Loss	0%	2%	8%
	(N)	(13)	(55)	(12)
		del_i = .00		

(*distance in scale steps: close = <1; moderate = 1; far = >1)
(**Easy Win = 60+% of the votes; Close Win = <60%)
Sources: 1978 CPS Study; Barone and Ujifosa, 1980.

ideologically close to their constituencies, 31% of those who were close had narrow victories, and 75% of those who were ideologically far from their constituencies had easy wins.

The association is no stronger when party, seniority, and closeness of prior race are controlled. Ideological deviation and reelection result correlate but .04 for Democrats, and -.09 for Republicans (the negative correlation showing even less support for the hypothesis than would be expected by chance). The correlation is .06 for less senior representatives; −.04 for more senior representatives; .02 for those with narrow victories in their previous House race, and −.07 for those with easy victories in their previous race.[11] There is nothing in these results to suggest that the perceived ideological distance of the representative from his or her constituency has any effect on how well the representative will fare in a bid for reelection.

With general ideological deviation showing so little effect on reelection prospects, it seems unlikely that deviation in any specific issue area will have significant impact. Nevertheless, each area measured by seven-point scales in the 1978 CPS study is analyzed. The results of those analyses are summarized in Table 3–2.

No association in any control table for any of the issue areas shows statistically significant support for the hypothesis. Many correlations are not even in the hypothesized direction. No subsample among the representatives appears to be substantially more or less supportive than any other subsample.

The same type of analysis is carried out for 1980, with essentially the same result. For 1980, perceived policy distance from the constituency is measured for five issue areas: liberal/conservative ideology, government-guaranteed jobs, government aid to minorities, women's equality, and getting along with Russia. The degree of association between perceived distance and the vote in each of those issue is summarized in Table

TABLE 3–2   Perceived Policy Distance from the Constituency and Reelection
Results: del, Correlations, 1978

| | POLICY ISSUE AREAS | | | | |
Subsample	Guaranteed Jobs	Aid to Minorities	Medical Insurance	Women's Equality	Rights of Accused
Whole Sample	.06	-.01	-.02	.06	.10
Democrats	.06	-.03	-.03	-.01	.17
Republicans	.06	.03	-.02	.22	-.04
*Less Senior**	.04	-.02	-.05	.11	.13
*More Senior**	.08	-.01	.02	.04	.06
*Close Prior Win***	.03	-.14	-.10	.15	.14
*Easy Prior Win***	.07	.02	.02	.06	.08

(*Less Senior = 0-6 years seniority; More Senior, >6 years)
(**Close Prior Win is by <60%; Easy Win, by 60+%)
(Numbers in each group [Ns] listed in note 11)
Sources: 1978 CPS Study; Barone and Ujifosa, 1980.

3–3. For 1980, controls included the percentage for Reagan, in addition
to those for party, seniority, and previous (1978) vote.[12]

The 1980 results are not much more supportive of the hypothesis
than were the 1978 results. In specific issue areas—jobs, aid to
minorities, and so on—the correlations are insignificant and frequently
opposite to what was hypothesized. There is a statistically significant association between ideological distance and reelection result for the more

TABLE 3–3   Perceived Policy Distance from the Constituency and Reelection
Results: del, Correlations, 1980

| | POLICY ISSUE AREAS | | | | |
Subsample*	Ideology	Guaranteed Jobs	Aid to Minorities	Women's Equality	Get Along with Russia
Whole Sample	.14	.00	.09	.06	-.02
Democrats	.17	.15	.16	.08	.04
Republicans	.06	-.12	.02	-.02	-.07
Less Senior	-.03	-.12	-.06	.00	-.02
More Senior	.37***	.09	.17	.11	-.02
*More Liberal Dist.***	.09	-.02	.05	.10	.01
*More Cons. Dist.***	.24	.02	.14	-.02	-.07
Close Prior Win	.34	-.21	.24	.01	.01
Easy Prior Win	.08	.09	.11	.06	-.02

(*See notes to Table 3–2. See note 12 for N's.)
(**More Liberal District, <mean Reagan vote; More Conservative, > the mean)
(***Statistically significant at .05 level in hypothesized direction)
Sources: 1980 CPS Study; Barone and Ujifosa, 1982.

senior representatives. But that is the only statistically significant association among the 40 control tables. As one would expect to find one or two significant associations purely by chance, there is no reason to believe that the single significant correlation reflects any more than chance variation in sampling.

Overall, Tables 3–1, 3–2, and 3–3 do not show that representatives who deviate from their constituencies' policy preferences will suffer at the polls. The three tables show no more support for that hypothesis than would be expected by chance.

Constituencies' Opinions and Incumbents' Voting Records

The analysis is somewhat more complicated when the measure of policy deviation is based on differences between constituency opinion and the representative's voting record, rather than on differences as they are perceived by respondents in the district.

The most difficult initial problem is finding questions posed to respondents that are sufficiently similar to those posed to their representatives so that one can estimate what each constituency's opinion would be on the issue actually brought to a vote in the House of Representatives. For 1978, there were three such questions: one dealing with support for the ERA, one with support for a one-third tax cut, and one with liberal/conservative preferences. The comparable questions facing the representatives were whether to allow rescission of ratifications of the ERA, whether to pass the Kemp-Roth tax cuts, and how liberal or conservative to be on a series of votes over the whole session of Congress.

As noted above, the question dealing with the ERA that respondents were asked had nothing to do with rescission. However, it seems reasonable to estimate that if 60% or more of the respondents in a district favored the ERA, that constituency opinion would be opposed to allowing rescission. If 40% or less of the respondents were in favor of the ERA, it seems reasonable to estimate that constituency opinion would be in favor of allowing rescissions. If more than 40% and less than 60% favored the ERA, especially given our small numbers of respondents, constituency opinion is best classified as unclear.

If both the representative and the constituency favored rescission *or* if both opposed rescission, the representative is coded as voting with the constituency. If the representative voted in favor, but the constituency opposed, *or* if the representative voted against while the constituency was in favor, then the representative is coded as voting against the constituency. If the position of the constituency was unclear or the representative failed to vote or pair for or against rescission, the representative is coded as "neutral," that is, neither with nor against the constituency.[13]

A similar technique was used to measure whether representatives voted with their constituencies or against their constituencies on the proposed thirty percent tax cut (Kemp-Roth bill). Respondents were asked if they agreed with the following statement:

Federal income taxes should be cut by at least one third even if it means reducing military spending and cutting down on government services such as health and education.

That was not exactly the issue facing many representatives when they had to vote on Kemp-Roth. At least the supply-siders favoring Kemp-Roth did not expect that the proposed tax cut would reduce revenues; hence, they did not expect that cutting taxes would reduce spending or services. Still, substantial differences among constituencies are apparent for the question asked. It seems reasonable to expect that if a majority of respondents would favor the cut even if it meant cuts in services (and a few districts did have a majority take that position), then the constituency would probably favor Kemp-Roth. If two thirds or more of the respondents opposed a tax cut under those conditions, one might infer that the district would oppose Kemp-Roth. If more than half but less than two thirds opposed the tax cut, the district position on Kemp-Roth was coded as unclear. As with the ERA, each constituency's opinion is compared with the voting of its representative to determine whether the representative is coded as with, neutral, or against his or her constituency.

It is possible to measure the distance between constituency opinion and incumbent voting on a general liberal/conservative spectrum, but the technique needed is somewhat different than that used for votes on a specific issue. Constituency opinion can be estimated to be the position taken by the median respondent on the seven-point liberalism/conservatism scale. The representative's position can be estimated by using the ACA ratings for 1977-1978. Both estimates are standardized, and the absolute value of the difference between the two is used to measure the representative's ideological deviation from constituency opinion. For example, if a district is one standard deviation more conservative than the mean district, and its representative is two standard deviations less conservative than the mean representative, then the distance between the constituency's opinion and its representative's voting would be 3. The measure of distance is collapsed into three categories: close (distance = 0-.75), moderate (distance = .751-1.25), and far (distance = >1.25).

Table 3–4 shows how little impact voting with or against constituency opinion had on reelection results. Constituency/representative differences on the ERA, the tax cut, and ideological issues in general are shown separately.

Regardless of issue, differences between the constituency's opinion and its representative's voting have no effect on reelection results. House members who vote against their constituencies' opinions are no more likely to lose reelection bids than are those who vote with their con-

TABLE 3–4 Voting With or Against Constituency Opinion and Reelection Result: 1978

		DISTANCE FROM CONSTITUENCY ON ERA*		
		With	Neutral	Against
Reelection	Easy Win	95%	59%	87%
Result**	Close Win	5%	37%	11%
	Loss	0%	4%	2%
	(N)	(45)	(27)	(21)
			del₁ = .02	

		DISTANCE FROM CONSTITUENCY ON TAX CUT*		
		With	Neutral	Against
Reelection	Easy Win	86%	76%	80%
Result**	Close Win	11%	24%	18%
	Loss	3%	0%	4%
	(N)	(28)	(25)	(40)
			del₁ = .02	

		IDEOLOGICAL DISTANCE FROM CONSTITUENCY*		
		Close	Moderate	Far
Reelection	Easy Win	79%	73%	88%
Result**	Close Win	18%	23%	12%
	Loss	3%	4%	0%
	(N)	(33)	(26)	(34)
			del₁ = -.04	

(*see text for distinctions among categories)
(**Easy Win = 60+%; Close Win = <60%)
Sources: 1978 CPS Study; Barone and Ujifosa, 1980.

stituencies. Those who are ideologically far from their constituency's opinions actually do slightly better in reelection races than do those who are ideologically closer to their constituencies.

As Table 3–5 shows, controlling for party, seniority, and closeness of previous race does not disclose any support for the hypothesis.

Nor is the 1980 analysis any more supportive of the hypothesis. For 1980, the variables, in addition to deviation from the constituency on general ideology, are with or against the constituency on defense spending, with or against the constituency on control of oil and gas prices, with or against the constituency on a nuclear moratorium, and deviation from the constituency on conservation issues.[14]

Table 3–6 summarizes the correlations between deviation as measured by each of those variables and reelection results. As with the

TABLE 3–5   Voting with or against Constituency Opinion and Reelection Result: del₁ Correlations, 1978

	POLICY ISSUE AREA			(N)
Subsamples*	ERA	Tax Cut	Ideology	
Whole Sample	.02	.02	-.04	(93)
Democrats	.07	.08	-.07	(59)
Republicans	-.04	-.06	.02	(34)
Less Senior	.02	.02	-.07	(52)
More Senior	.04	.02	.01	(41)
Close Prior Win	.06	.02	.01	(30)
Easy Prior Win	-.03	.00	-.01	(63)

(*See notes to Table 3–2)
(No coefficient significant at .05 level in hypothesized direction)
Sources: 1978 CPS Study; Barone and Ujifosa, 1980.

earlier 1980 analyses, control variables are party, seniority, previous vote, and 1980 percentage for Reagan.

The associations are about what one would expect if there were no association between the measures of policy deviation and reelection results. There are actually more associations in the wrong direction than in the hypothesized direction. When the policy deviation of the incumbent from his or her constituency is measured by whether the incumbent is voting with or against public opinion, there is no evidence that deviation lessens reelection prospects.

TABLE 3–6   Voting with or against Constituency Opinion and Reelection Result: del₁ Correlations, 1980

	POLICY ISSUE AREA					(N)
Subsamples*	Defense Spending	Oil & Gas	Nuclear Moratorium	Conser- vation	Ideo- logy	
Whole Sample	.11	-.07	-.02	-.12	-.07	(91)
Democrats	.11	-.04	.01	-.14	-.02	(56)
Republicans	.10	-.05	-.02	-.10	.00	(35)
Less Senior	.14	-.11	-.03	-.13	-.06	(48)
More Senior	.07	-.03	.01	-.11	.02	(41)
More Liberal Dist.	.07	.00	.04	-.10	-.02	(44)
More Cons. Dist.	.17	-.16	-.08	-.15	-.05	(47)
Close Prior Win	.14	-.12	-.06	-.23	.04	(23)
Easy Prior Win	.08	-.03	.02	-.10	.01	(68)

(*See notes to Table 3–3)
(No coefficient significant at .05 level in hypothesized direction)
Sources: 1980 CPS Study; Barone and Ujifosa, 1982.

Constituency/Representative Voting Differences

It is possible that the analyses above have failed to uncover support for the hypothesis because of their reliance on survey data or because the use of ordinal-level measurement understated the strength of association. The more standard analysis shown below relates interval-level measures based on voting behavior.

As noted earlier, the measure of policy distance is the absolute value of the differences in the standardized scores for the liberalism of the constituency and the liberalism of the representative. The measure of the probability of reelection is the percent of the vote won by the incumbent. Table 3–7 shows the Pearson's r correlation between the two variables for 1984 (the only year for which the measures could be calculated). Both the bivariate correlation and the partial correlations, controlling for party, seniority, and percentage of vote in previous race, are reported.

The hypothesis suggests a negative association between distance and probability of reelection, and that association, as reported in Table 3–7, is indeed negative. However, it is very weak—accounting for less than 0.5 percent of the variance in support—and is just barely significant once the other variables are controlled.

This fairly standard way of testing the hypothesis shows no more support for it than did the earlier tests. From none of these tests is there evidence that policy deviation affects reelection prospects. It appears that once elected, almost all members of Congress continue to get reelected, barring extreme old age, illness, scandal, reapportionment, or other catastrophic event.[15] A few do lose, and several more have close calls each year. But these analyses show that losses and the close calls cannot be systematically traced back to how far the members' policies deviate from the policies favored by their constituencies. There was virtually no association found between policy deviation and margin of victory. Defeats and close calls seem to afflict those who vote with their

TABLE 3–7   Regression Analysis: Ideological Distance, Party, Seniority, Previous Vote, and Probability of Reelection, 1984

Variable	Correlation	Partial Correlation	Regression Coefficient
Ideological Distance	-.06	-.09	-1.9
Party (R = 1; D = 0)	.00	.15*	3.7
Seniority (years)	.13*	-.04	-.07
Previous Vote Percentage	.59*	.60*	.66

(N=390)
(* significant at the .05 level)
Sources: Barone and Ujifosa, 1986; Congressional Quarterly, 1987.

constituents' wishes just about as often as they afflict those who vote against their constituents' wishes.

BOUNDING THE HYPOTHESIS

It is tempting at this point simply to conclude that constituencies do not behave as the myth of constituency control would suggest. Certainly, there is no support for the hypothesis underlying the myth as that hypothesis is normally stated, regardless of whether it is tested in the standard fashion or through use of survey data. Nevertheless, the theoretical arguments and evidence regarding the comparative nature of evaluation presented in the last chapter suggest that the weak or non-existent support for the hypothesis found in this and other studies may be a consequence of failing to specify properly the circumstances to which the hypothesis applies, and not a consequence of constituencies' ignoring all policy deviation.

Figure 3–1 shows the standard association that is hypothesized to exist between distance from the constituency, graphed as the X-axis, and support for the incumbent, graphed as the Y-axis. Distance from the constituency is measured directionally (the incumbent is so many units to the right or left of the constituency), rather than in absolute units.

The assertion is that the farther the incumbent is to the left or right of the constituency preference, the less support the constituency will give in the reelection race. If support is measured in percentage of the vote, the expectation is that at some distance to the left and right of the constituency, support will drop below 50%. In testing the hypothesis as usually stated, it is standard to use absolute values of the distance because the direction of the distance is not relevant (Wright, 1977; Johannes and McAdams, 1981; Whitby and Bledsoe, 1986).

FIGURE 3–1 Standard Hypothesized Association between Distance from the Constituency and Support for the Incumbent

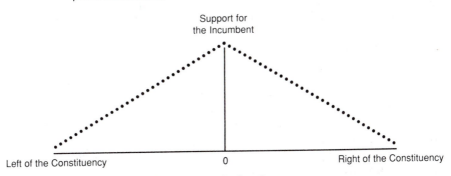

Support for
the Incumbent

Left of the Constituency   0   Right of the Constituency

Distance from the Constituency

The findings of the last chapter, however, were that direction of deviation is important to the voter, and that the voter responds differently to the direction of deviation by incumbents of different parties. It was hypothesized, and verified for at least some voters, that Republican incumbents can deviate to the left and Democratic incumbents can deviate to the right without provoking a loss of support among the knowledgeable voters. The argument was made in that chapter that deviation is evaluated relative to what would have been expected by an alternative representative—in the general election, to what would be expected by a representative of the other party. Republicans seen as too far left are not punished because they deviated less than a Democrat presumably would have. Similarly, voters do not punish a Democrat seen as too far right, for a Republican would have been worse.

If the logic and findings of Chapter 2 are correct, in the general election the hypothesis will only hold for Republicans to the right of their constituency and for Democrats to the left of theirs. The hypothesis should be restricted to read: *In general elections, among Republicans to the right of their constituencies and Democrats to the left of their constituencies*, the farther members of Congress deviate from the policy preferences of their constituencies, the greater is the probability of their defeat. Figure 3–2 shows the expected associations between policy distance and support for the incumbent under the bounded hypothesis *for incumbents of each party*.

If the bounded hypothesis is correct, four separate regressions should be run: one each for Republicans to the left, Republicans to the right, Democrats to the left, and Democrats to the right of their respective constituency's preference. The measure of distance need not be the absolute value of the difference, but simply the difference, between the liberalism of the constituency and the liberalism of the representative (thus, positive differences show the representative to the right of the constituency; negative scores show the representative to the left). With such a directional measure of distance, as the graphs in Figure 3–2 show, the direction and magnitude of the correlations between distance and support would be expected to vary: negative for Republicans to the right, positive for Democrats to the left, and zero for the other two groups of incumbents.

If evaluations of distance are relative, far different bounds for the hypothesis are suggested when it is applied to primary races rather than general elections. In the general election, Republican incumbents who have been to the left of their constituencies are protected by the perception that the only viable alternatives would probably have been even further left. That protection does not exist in the Republican primary. Incumbents who have been to the left of the constituency as a whole have almost certainly been even further to the left of those voting in the Republican primary, and the perception is likely to be that *other*

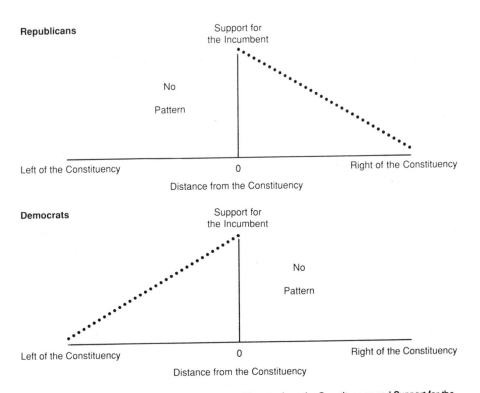

FIGURE 3–2 Hypothesized Associations Between Distance from the Constituency and Support for the Incumbent: By Party, for General Elections

Republicans would not have been as far left. The further Republican incumbents have deviated to the left of their constituencies, the more certain primary voters are to feel that another Republican would have done better, and the lower their support is likely to be for the incumbent.

In contrast, policy distance is unlikely to affect support in the primaries for Republican incumbents who have deviated to the right of their constituencies. First, since the voters in the Republican primary tend to prefer policies to the right of those preferred by the constituency as a whole, an incumbent who has deviated to the right may be seen as fairly close to the preferences of the voters. Second, voters have no easy guide from party labels and past party performance to judge whether others in the primary race would probably have been further away from their preferences than was the incumbent. Unlike Republican incumbents to the left of the constituency, Republicans to the right will not be typically viewed as further from voter preferences than would be their opponents. In specific races incumbents might be punished for policy deviation, but there should be no general pattern, so there should be little or no overall association between distance and support.

Analogous reasoning suggests that the further Democrats deviate to the right of their constituencies, the lower their support is likely to be in the Democratic primaries. Democrats to the left of their constituencies, however, are unlikely to be affected in the primaries by the extent of their deviation.

A second restricted hypothesis can then be stated: *in primary elections, among Republicans to the left of their constituency and Democrats to the right of their constituencies*, the further members of Congress deviate from the policy preferences of their constituencies, the greater is the probability of their defeat. Figure 3–3 shows the expected associations between policy distance and support for the incumbent under the bounded hypothesis for incumbents of each party.

The patterns expected for incumbents of the two parties has reversed from the general elections to the primaries. Four regressions can also be run to test this hypothesis, with the expection being that distance and support will correlate positively for Republicans to the left of their constituency, negatively for Democrats to the right, and not at all for the other two classes of incumbents.

FIGURE 3–3   Hypothesized Associations between Distance from the Constituency and Support for the Incumbent: By Party, for Primary Elections

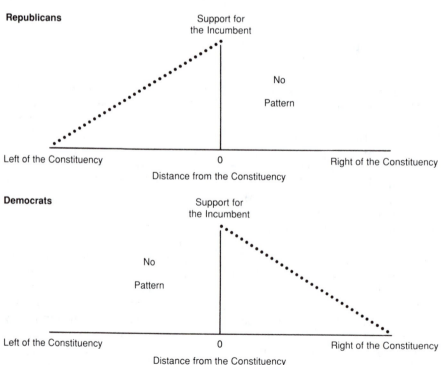

TESTING THE BOUNDED HYPOTHESIS

Table 3–8 shows the Pearson's r correlations, bivariate and partial, between ideological distance and support for the incumbent for both the general election and the primaries, 1984. The partial correlations control for seniority and percentage of vote in previous race.

The results reported in Table 3–8 are strongly supportive of the bounded hypothesis. The projected positive associations are significantly positive; the negatives, negative; and the zeros, quite close to zero. The associations are not strong, accounting for 6-16% of the variance in support in the groups where distance does have an effect. Nevertheless, there is finally evidence that deviation from the policy preferences of one's constituents can cost the incumbent support, at least under certain specified circumstances.

The results reported in Table 3–8 show the importance of bounding the hypothesis. As traditionally stated, the hypothesis is not applicable to about 30% of the incumbents in the general election and 70% of the incumbents in the primaries. Traditional analyses, including the regression analysis reported in Table 3–7, have only found weak to nearly nonexistent support for the hypothesis because it is weakly supported for

TABLE 3–8   Correlation Coefficients between Ideological Distance and Probability of Reelection: By Party and Direction of Deviation, 1984

	Hypothesized Correlation	r	Partial r	Regression Coefficient**	(N)
General Election					
Republicans— Left of District	0	-.09	-.07	-2.3	(41)
Republicans— Right of District	-	-.40*	-.35*	-9.0	(108)
Democrats— Left of District	+	.27*	.22*	6.2	(165)
Democrats— Right of District	0	.25	.01	.1	(77)
Primary Elections					
Republicans— Left of District	+	.30*	.30*	8.6	(41)
Republicans— Right of District	0	.00	.02	.4	(108)
Democrats— Left of District	0	-.01	-.02	-.4	(165)
Democrats— Right of District	-	-.24*	-.31*	-6.4	(79)

(* significant at .05 level)
(** from multiple regression equation)
Sources: Barone and Ujifosa, 1986; Congressional Quarterly, 1987.

some groups of representatives and not at all for others. When the groups are mixed together, one gets very weak to nearly nonexistent support.

The relative nature of incumbent evaluations that suggested the bounds for the hypothesis also offers an explanation for why Wright (1977) found that Republican, but not Democratic, supporters of Nixon were punished (albeit, weakly). In evaluating Republican Nixon supporters, voters were likely to think that a Democrat would not have done as badly. In evaluating Democratic Nixon supporters, voters were likely to think a Republican would have been at least as bad.

THE DECISIVENESS OF DEVIATION

As noted in the last chapter, there are two ways in which policy distance from the constituency might be decisive in a reelection race: (1) incumbents might have lost by such small margins that had they been positioned closer to the preferred position, they might have picked up enough support to have won the elections; (2) incumbents might have won by such small margins that had they been positioned further from the preferred position, they might have lost enough support to have lost the elections. The data reported in Table 3–8 can be used to estimate how many representatives were in either of those situations in 1984.

In the general elections, the insignificant associations between distance and support for Republicans to the left and Democrats to the right of the constituency indicate that distance from the constituency could not have been decisive for any of those representatives. In contrast, distance was significant for Republicans to the right and Democrats to the left of the constituency. The regression coefficients presented in Table 3–8 indicate that Republicans to the right of the constituency lost an estimated 9% in support for every standard deviation that they were positioned to the right; Democrats to the left lost an estimated 6.2% for every standard deviation that they were positioned to the left.

It is easy to use the regression coefficients to estimate whether a position right at the constituency preference would have picked up enough votes for an incumbent to have won. For example, if a Republican were one standard deviation to the right of his or her constituency and got 42% of the vote, the regression coefficient indicates that if that incumbent had been positioned right at the constituency preference, he or she would probably have picked up another 9% of the vote for a total of 51% and the win. In 1984 there were nine Democrats far enough to the left and one Republican far enough to the right of their constituencies' preferences who lost by a small enough margin for the regression coefficient to indicate that they probably would have won had they been positioned right at their constituencies' preferences.

It is harder to use the regression coefficients to count the races in which positioning was necessary for a win. One might argue that if each standard deviation to the right of the constituency cost a Republican 9%, then being near the constituency preference was necessary even for an incumbent who got 70% of the vote—for that candidate could not have afforded to have been positioned three standard deviations to the right without losing the election. Such an argument is predicated on an impossible condition: In 1984, one standard deviation equalled 32.6 in the ACA ratings; thus it probably was impossible on the ACA scale, with its 100 maximum, for an incumbent to be three standard deviations to the right of his or her constituency.

One standard for judging decisiveness is to postulate that any incumbent who was more than one standard deviation (almost one third of the political spectrum) from the preferred position of the constituency and still won did so in spite of his or her ideology. (75% of all Republicans to the right and Democrats to the left of their constituencies were within one standard deviation of the preferred position.) One could then estimate from the regression coefficient whether each of those who were less than a standard deviation from the preferred ideology would have won had they been positioned a full standard deviation from the preferred ideology. That is done by subtracting the actual deviation of each incumbent from 1, multiplying the resulting fraction by the regression coefficient, and subtracting that answer from the percentage of the vote won. If the result is less than 50%, positioning was decisive for that incumbent. Thus, if an incumbent was one fourth a standard deviation away from the preferred ideology and he or she won by less than three fourths of the regression coefficient, positioning was decisive in the win. Using that standard, there were two Republicans and five Democrats whose wins in 1984 were so narrow that their positioning was decisive.

Combining those 7 races with the 10 races in which positioning was apparently decisive in losing gives a total of 17 out of 390 races in the general election in which one might argue that policy deviation from the constituency was critical in determining whether or not an incumbent was reelected.

The same analysis can be performed for the primary elections. In those elections, losses were less frequent, wins were generally by a large margin, and the hypothesis applied to only about 30% of all races (Republicans to the left and Democrats to the right of their constituencies). It is not surprising, then, that ideological distance from the constituency was rarely decisive. It was decisive for no Republican, as no Republican to the left of his or her constituency won less than 62% of the vote in a primary. It was decisive for five Democrats: three who won narrowly, and two who lost narrowly. Even if the standard of winning narrowly is extended to those who would have lost if they were two standard deviations from the preferred ideology (because Democrats did deviate substantially to the right of the preferred ideology in their districts), ideological distance was decisive in only one more primary race.

CONCLUSION

This chapter looked at evidence testing the hypothesis that the more the policies voted for by the incumbent differ from those favored by his or her constituency, the lower the probability that the incumbent will get reelected. Stated that broadly, there was little support for the hypothesis. There was, however, support for bounded versions of the hypothesis. The bounds were determined by the positioning of the representative relative to likely alternative representatives, that is, relative to members of the opposition party in the general election and to members of the same party in the primaries.

In general elections, Republican incumbents to the right and Democratic incumbents to the left of their constituencies (about 70% of all incumbents) tended to receive a lower percentage of the vote the further they deviated from the preferred ideology of their constituency. In the primaries, the remaining incumbents (Republicans to the left and Democrats to the right of their constituencies) tended to receive lower percentages of the vote the further they deviated from the constituency preference.

In either case, policy distance from the constituency had a statistically significant but weak impact on voter support. An analysis of how decisive that impact was in winning or losing disclosed 17 general election races and 5 primary races in 1984 in which the policy distance was probably decisive.

The results regarding the decisiveness of policy distance obtained from analysis of constituency voting in 1984 do not differ much from those obtained by the analysis of individual voting in 1980 discussed in the previous chapter. Distance from the preferred ideology of the constituency, at least in fairly high turnover years, is likely to cost 2-3% of the House members their jobs. Staying close to the preferred ideology probably protects another 2-3% who might otherwise lose theirs.

These findings can be read in two very different ways. One could emphasize how unlikely it is that the positions an incumbent has adopted will decide a reelection bid. It seems clear that nearly all members of Congress can behave as free agents on virtually all issues with little fear of voter retaliation or promise of voter reward. Alternatively, one could emphasize that members have their jobs on the line, and that there is some chance that the policies they have adopted will determine whether they return to Congress. Constituencies may not reward and punish very often, but the knowledge that they do so even occasionally may be enough to maintain constituency control over Congress.

Either reading emphasizes the general pattern. Even those who emphasize the free agency of members would concede that there may be a specific issue that is so important to a given district that a representative is not free to vote for or against it without electoral consequence. And those who emphasize control over the member would concede that there are some issues where control cannot be effective because the issue is too remote or the constituency position is unknown.

Whether members *do* behave as free agents or whether they tend to bow to the preferences of their constituencies is investigated in the next chapter. What this and the last chapters have shown is that it is *possible* for members to behave as free agents on broad issues of policy without severely damaging their reelection prospects.

NOTES

[1]That assumption might be justified by the argument that conservative Republicans and liberal Democrats represent their parties' "ideological extremes" and are likely to be far from the median voter preference, which tends to be near the "middle of the political spectrum" (Erikson, 1971: 1018). Erikson suggests (1971: 1018) that his work might be read as a test of whether members of Congress are "rewarded and punished at the polls on the basis of their performance."

[2]The assumption that district preference is a linear function of the liberal vote for president seems to somewhat assume what is to be proved. Preferred ADA score was computed to be -20 + 1.8 (% McGovern).

[3]Getting all three measures for the same year was impossible for Johannes and McAdams because (a) they needed a year in which there was a conservative/liberal contest for president with no third candidate in order to measure district liberalism, but (b) they needed a year with little redistricting so that the reelection would take place in essentially the same district as the previous election. No year for which ADA records were available met both criteria before 1984.

[4]Spatial analysis suggests the median difference to be more critical than the mean difference (Bernstein, 1976).

[5]Numbers (Ns) vary slightly from scale to scale.

[6]As Bond, et al., (1984) argue, the ACA ratings are preferable to the ADA rating because the ACA does not equate missed votes with opposition.

[7]The comparative measures of policy deviation are:

using standard scores: $| Z_R - Z_C |$

using residual scores: $\sigma_R | Z_R - rZ_C |$

(where Z_R = standardized liberalism score for the representative; Z_C = standardized liberalism score for the constituency; δ_R = the standard deviation of the liberalism scores for the representatives, and r = the Pearson's correlation coefficient between the two measures of liberalism.)

As the first equation indicates, using standard scores, the relative liberalism of the representatives and the constituencies are equally weighted. In contrast, as the second equation indicates, using residual scores would reduce the weight given to constituency liberalism by multiplying the score for such liberalism by a fraction equal to r. For 1984, when $r = .61$, using residual scores would have weighted the relative liberalism of the representative more than 1.6 times as heavily as the relative liberalism of the constituency.

[8]Excluded are representatives whose districts have been significantly altered between 1982 and 1984 (thus excluding all of New Jersey). Also excluded are races apparently determined by sex scandals or felony convictions.

[9]One person who did not see ideology as decisive in the 1984 race was Geraldine Ferraro. See her statements on *Good Morning America*, Oct. 22, 1985.

[10]For a detailed discussion of the del_1 correlation coefficient, see Bernstein and Dyer (1984). Del_1 is interpretable as a proportional-reduction-in-error (P-R-E) measure, where the magnitude of the coefficient equals the proportion fewer observed deviations from perfect association than would be expected by chance. A zero del_1 indicates no fewer errors than would be expected by chance. Del_1 is preferable to other P-R-E measures, such as gamma, in not being inflated by around-the-corner associations. Choice of correlation coefficient makes no real difference in these analyses; for comparison, gamma for Table 3-1 is -.06.

[11]There were 80 in the whole sample: 48 Democrats, 32 Republicans; 43 less senior, 37 more senior; 28 with close prior wins, 52 with easy prior wins. The tables include incumbent races in which there was major-party competition. Those races are important theoretically. If candidates far from their constituents do not even attract challengers, that weighs heavily against the hypothesis. Similarly, if those close to their constituents do not attract challengers, that weighs strongly in support of the hypothesis. Certainly the 100% - 0% races should be classified with the other easy wins. Some, however, may argue that if those representatives had had competition, they might not have had such easy wins— they might even have been held to less than 60% of the vote—and therefore, uncontested races should be excluded from the analysis. I do not agree; I think it very unlikely that incumbents who ran uncontested races would have had close wins or losses if challenged. Nevertheless, I have computed the bivariate correlations without the uncontested races and no correlation coefficient changes by more than .03, and the changes do not generally strengthen the hypothesis. The correlation for Table 3-1, for example, remains at .00 with uncontested races eliminated.

[12]N's for Table 3-3: whole sample, 53; Democrats, 30; Republicans, 23; less senior, 25; more senior, 28; more liberal, 23; more conservative, 30; close win, 15; easy win, 38.

[13]In the rare instance when the representative did not take a position on the bill and the constituency was undecided, the representative was also coded 1, that is, "with" his or her constituency.

[14] Constituency opinion was derived from CPS questions on whether defense spending should be increased or decreased; government should continue to control oil and gas prices; government should build any more nuclear power plants; and whether government should relax environmental protection regulations. The comparable positions for the representatives are taken from key votes reported in Barone and Ujifosa (1982) on defense spending, oil and gas decontrol, a six-month moratorium on nuclear plant construction permits, and the League of Conservation Voters' evaluation of voting on conservation issues and the ACA's evaluation of general ideology.

[15]This study does not investigate the possibility that deviation may "catch up with" an incumbent over time, that policy deviation from the constituency will reduce reelection probabilities over a series of elections. A test of that hypothesis has yet to be published, but the theory behind it is not convincing. If the people do not turn out a deviant congressman at one of the first few opportunities, how likely is it that they will do so in later races? Data indicate that incumbents tend to be safer in later races than they were in their first attempts at reelection (Bond, 1985).

FOUR

Assumptions Regarding Members of Congress

The last two chapters have uncovered the weak underpinnings of the myth that constituencies control congressional behavior: Citizens rarely know of and respond to policies supported by their representatives, and constituencies rarely reward or punish incumbents on the basis of how far they have deviated from policies favored by those constituencies. However, the ultimate test of constituency control must be found in the behavior of the members of Congress. Do they generally act as though they were controlled by their constituencies? When there is a conflict between what their own ideology dictates and what their constituencies want, do members vote the wishes of their constituencies?

As noted in Chapter 1, it is meaningless to talk about constituency *control* unless one observes instances when the representative is crosspressured: when the member's own ideology (or party or presidential pressures) would suggest casting one vote, while constituency pressure would suggest casting another. Everyone expects substantial *coincidence* between congressional voting and constituency opinion. After all, members are generally long-term residents of their constituencies and were selected by those constituencies to serve in the Congress. On most issues, members are likely to have the same views as their constituencies. *Constituency control* is evident only when crosspressured members bow to the wishes of their constituencies.

THE CASE FOR CONSTITUENCY CONTROL

In light of the evidence presented in the last two chapters, some may wonder why anyone would expect to find evidence of constituency control over congressional voting. Constituents generally do not know the policy positions taken by their representatives; often they do not cast their votes on the basis of those positions when they do know them. The reelection prospects for members of Congress are about the same regardless of how far they deviate from their constituencies on policies or on general ideology. Why, then, expect members to alter their votes to please their constituents?

One reason for expecting control is that members of Congress might *anticipate* an electoral payoff for voting with their constituencies and modify their voting to get that payoff—*even though such a payoff was not being offered.* Though the evidence shows that modifying their voting has no payoff, members may behave as though it does. Virtually everyone who has studied Congressional voting can cite members who claim to be worried about the electoral impact of votes in Congress (see, e.g., Stokes and Miller, 1962; Kingdon, 1973).

The case for constituency control does not rest on the (unfounded) *anticipation* of electoral payoffs. For members worried about reelection, the safest course of action would be to vote with their constituencies *just in case* there are electoral payoffs.

Even though more than 90% of them are reelected each year, Weissberg (1981) claims that members of Congress are very worried about their reelection prospects. The apparently inexplicable defeats of some of their "safe" colleagues cause high levels of anxiety among the rest. Members "run scared." They are afraid of giving constituents any reason for voting against them. Since voting with the constituency can hardly be held against a member, "playing it safe" will incline members to vote with their constituencies.

Furthermore, as Wright (1978) argues, policy deviation from the constituency is one of the few factors potentially relevant to reelection that is within the control of each member. National tides, age, the economy, concurrent presidential, senatorial, and gubernatorial races, party registration, immigration, and a host of other factors might influence prospects for reelection—but most of those are beyond the control of the member. One of the few things members *can* do is decrease deviation from their constituencies on policy issues. Such decreases might not enhance reelection prospects. But just in case they do, members might be expected to prefer decreasing policy deviation to just sitting and waiting for whatever the fates may bring.

Concerns over reelection are not the only reason for expecting constituency control over congressional voting. As Kingdon (1973: 46) notes, while in office members "are constantly called upon to explain to constituents why they voted as they did." Voting against constituency wishes causes much more harassment than voting with their wishes. Members might be expected to vote with their constituencies simply to avoid the trouble of explaining why they voted the "wrong" way.

A final reason for expecting some constituency control over congressional voting is that some members of Congress may believe that they *ought to represent* their constituencies, regardless of their own preferences on issues. While it is unclear just how many members of Congress see themselves as "instructed delegates" for their constituencies, surveys of legislators at the state and national level show that many claim to function in that manner (see, e.g., Eulau, et al., 1959; Kuklinski and McCrone, 1981).

Thus, despite the evidence regarding individuals and constituencies shown in the last two chapters, it is possible to make a logical case for constituency control over Congressional voting. Much of that case, however, is built on what members tell us about why they vote as they do. For a number of reasons, what they tell us is suspect.

To start with, it is doubtful that very many politicians would openly state that they ignore their constituents or that they take reelection for granted. Some members may knowingly ignore their constituencies' preferences, but they are unlikely to tell us about it.

Additionally, some members, unsure of what their constituents actually favor, may project onto their constituencies their own policy positions. Or selective perception of communications from their constituents may lead members to think they are modifying their own positions to accommodate their constituents when they are, in fact, accommodating only a minority of those constituents. Hence, some members may honestly think they are voting their constituents' wishes when they are not (Maass, 1983).

Finally, some members may bow to constituency pressure occasionally, but they may fail to realize how infrequently they do so when they think the constituency is wrong. They may repress memories of conflicts with constituents or they may rationalize that "the constituents would have voted" as the representatives voted if only the constituents had known what the representatives knew. Thus, for a variety of reasons, members may overreport the frequency with which they bow to constituency influence.

For evidence regarding the extent of constituency control, one has to go beyond congressional expressions of concern with constituency opinion to look at members' actual voting patterns.

EVIDENCE REGARDING CONSTITUENCY CONTROL

Much of what passes for evidence of constituency control does not get to the heart of the issue: whether representatives generally bow to the wishes of their constituents when those wishes are in conflict with the representatives' own (or with other pressures on the representative).

At one time, what passed for evidence was nothing more than a collection of anecdotes. Senator Henry "Scoop" Jackson was known as "the Senator from Boeing." National defense votes were considered "real estate" decisions, where the major concerns were which district got which base. Energy votes were assumed to be so responsive to constituency pressures that Robert Engler (1964: 397) could contend that it "is difficult to find a congressman from an oil or gas state who will ever vote 'wrong' on oil or gas legislation."

Of course, one could always find anecdotes that refuted the assumption of constituency influence. For example, on a tight vote over whether to fund research and development on the ABM (anti-ballistic missile), the opposition to funding was led by Senator Clifford Case (Rep.) of New Jersey—the state that was to receive the prime contract for the ABM if the legislation passed. Along similar lines, Representative Bob Eckhardt (Dem.) of Texas (a gas-producing state) consistently opposed natural gas deregulation while Senator James Buckley (Cons.) of New York (a gas-consuming state) led the fight for its adoption.

Going beyond the anecdotes, a number of researchers have found evidence of generally weak bivariate associations between constituencies' wishes (or variables that might serve as surrogates for constituencies' wishes) and congressional voting behavior (see, for example, Turner, 1951; Froman, 1963; Shannon, 1968; Russett, 1970; Clotfelter, 1970; Moyer, 1973; Clausen, 1973; MacRae, 1976; Cobb, 1976; Ray, 1981; Hurley, 1982). However, those bivariate associations do not constitute evidence of constituency control. To constitute evidence of control, the associations between constituencies' wishes and Congressional voting must be shown to hold after controlling for the effects of members' personal ideology.

There are now more than 15 studies that have looked at the effect of constituencies' wishes on Congressional behavior while controlling for the effect of personal ideology (and occasionally other factors). The rest of this chapter reports the findings of those studies.[1]

MEASURING DEGREE OF CONSTITUENCY CONTROL

Constituency control is evident to the extent that members' votes deviate from what would have been expected on the basis of their own ideology (and other factors) to conform better to what would be expected if they were voting to please their constituencies. Thus, any study that hopes to find evidence of constituency control must measure three variables: (1) how each member would be expected to vote if motivated by his or her own ideology (and, possibly, other nonconstituency factors); (2) how each member would be expected to vote if motivated by his or her constituency; and (3) how each member actually did vote. Where the ideologically-motivated vote and the constituency-motivated vote would be expected to differ, observing the actual vote will determine which was the stronger motivation.

There are basically two ways of measuring the independent variables, that is, the categories from which ideological and constituency motivation can be inferred. One is to dichotomize those variables: ideological and constituency preferences are each classified as either favoring or opposing a particular vote.

Alternatively, those variables can be measured continuously. Ideological and constituency preferences are then measured by scales that might, for example, go from 0 to 100; the higher the number, the more pressure to vote for a particular position.

Using Dichotomous Variables

Treating the independent variables as dichotomies allows for a four-fold classification of representatives: (1) those whose ideology and constituency favor the vote, (2) those whose ideology favors, but whose constituency opposes, (3) those whose ideology and constituency oppose the vote, and (4) those whose ideology opposes, but whose constituency favors. Evidence regarding the extent of constituency control comes from comparing the behavior of the crosspressured members and non-crosspressured members (comparing those in group 2 with those in group 1, those in group 4 with those in group 3). To the extent that those crosspressured members cast a higher percentage of the votes suggested by their constituencies (oppose for group 2, favor for group 4), there is evidence of constituency control.

Suppose, for example, there was a vote on whether to expand a program transferring income from the rich to the poor. Members might be classified as liberal (ideologically motivated to favor the expansion) or conservative (ideologically motivated to oppose the expansion). Members might futher be classified as representing poor districts (constituency motivated to favor the expansion) or representing wealthier districts (constituency motivated to oppose expansion). Liberals representing wealthier districts and conservatives representing poor districts would be crosspressured. If 90% of the liberals representing poor districts favored expanding the program and just 20% of the liberals representing wealthier districts favored expansion, the 70% difference could be attributed to the control the constituencies were exerting over their representatives. If 90% of the conservatives representing wealthier districts opposed expansion and 90% (or more) of the conservatives representing poor districts also opposed expansion, there would be no evidence that the constituencies had any control over their representatives.

The analysis would be similar if an index, rather than a single vote, were used to measure voting in a particular issue area. One would compare the index for crosspressured members to the index for noncrosspressured representatives and attribute the difference to the effect of constituency pressure.

Using dichotomous independent variables leads to a very straightforward analysis of whether constituency control is strong enough to cause crosspressured representatives to abandon their own preferences to vote the preferences of their constituencies.

Using Continuous Variables

Dichotomizing the independent variables may, however, oversimplify the nature of ideological and constituency pressures. Ideological preference may strongly or weakly suggest a particular vote. Similarly, strength of constituency preference may vary. A second methodological approach is to treat the independent variables as continuous.

When both variables are treated as continuous, there is no fourfold classification of representatives. Each member may be crosspressured to a different extent than every other member. Hence, the data presentation and interpretation is less straightforward. An analysis has to be used that measures the extent to which voting reflects strength of constituency pressure after the effects of ideological pressure have been taken into account. The better the measure of constituency pressure predicts the voting behavior of the representatives, once the ideological (and other) variables have predicted as best they can, the stronger the evidence of constituency influence.

Suppose, for example, an index were developed of how supportive each member was of programs transferring money from the rich to the poor. Suppose further that members' ideologies were rated on a scale of 0 (most conservative) to 100 (most liberal), and the median family incomes of the constituencies they represented were coded in dollars. One might then use a regression equation to predict the transfer-program index scores from the ideological ratings. Presumably, higher index scores would be associated with higher ratings, but the association would not be perfect. For example, if constituency pressure also affects voting, a member representing a very poor district would tend to be higher on the index than would be predicted simply from his or her ideological rating. One could use a partial correlation coefficient to measure the extent to which the median family income represented by a member could predict the imperfections in the association between the ideological ratings and the index. The higher the correlation coefficient, the greater the extent of constituency influence.

Using continuous, rather than dichotomous, measures of the independent variables increases precision in measuring constituency *in-*

fluence, but somewhat obscures measurement of the extent of constituency *control*. Correlation coefficients can indicate shifts from ideologically motivated positions in the direction of constituency preferences, but they cannot indicate how often those shifts went so far as to cause representatives to vote against their own preferences (Achen, 1977; Jones, 1981).

INFERRING CONSTITUENCY AND IDEOLOGICAL PREFERENCES

There are two types of data sources for constituency-motivated and ideologically-motivated preferences on issues. The most commonly-used method is to infer those preferences from other properties of the representatives and their constituencies. Alternatively, one can ask representatives what their personal preferences are and what they believe their constituencies' preferences to be.

Inferring Preferences from Constituency Characteristics

Constituencies' attitudes on proposed legislation are typically inferred from the economic gain or loss that would accrue to each constituency from the passage of that legislation. No inference is certain, but it seems likely that constituencies will favor legislation that will profit them and oppose legislation that will cost them. This technique may not perfectly identify constituencies' positions, but inferring their positions from economic circumstances seems no more risky than inferring them from members' perceptions or from surveys of a small number of respondents within each constituency.

It has occasionally been possible to infer constituency preferences from noneconomic characteristics. Inferences have been made from public opinion polls (McCormick and Black, 1983), from hunting licenses per capita (Vedlitz, 1983), and from constituency membership in environmental groups (Kalt and Zupan, 1984). Substantive results appear to be fairly similar whether inferences were made from economic or noneconomic characteristics.

Inferring Preferences from Other Voting

Members' personal preferences on the issues are typically inferred from voting on issues other than the proposed legislation. Inferring members' ideologies from voting on other issues is also uncertain, but researchers do have the security of basing their inferences on a behavioral record of how conservative or liberal each member has been on a wide range of issues. A number of organizations publish ideology ratings based on congressional voting, saving researchers the necessity of constructing their own indexes.[2]

One objection that might be raised to inferring ideology from standard ratings is that those ratings may not measure the personal ideology of representatives, but instead "serve as a proxy for constituents' . . . economic interests" (Kalt 1981: 268).[3] In other words, ADA scores might reflect representatives' past efforts to please their constituents, rather than "altruistic" personal ideologies. A liberal ADA score might not be the consequence of liberal convictions, but a facade designed to please voters. If that were the case, ADA ratings would just be indirect measures of constituency influence. Finding correlations between ADA ratings and voting while controlling for more direct measures of constituency influence would not show ideological motivation to be stronger than constituency motivation; it would simply show that constituency influence was indirect.

Two sets of economists have thoroughly tested the validity of making ideological inferences from standardized scores (Kau and Rubin, 1982; Kalt, 1981; Kalt and Zupan, 1984). One method of testing was to use two-stage analyses, in the first stage of which various indicators of constituencies' interests were allowed to account for as much variation in the standardized scores as they could.[4] At that first stage, party was also allowed to account for as much variation in the standard scores as it could. The researchers then created "residual" measures, variations in standard scores that were peculiar to each senator and could not be explained away as proxies for virtually any measure of constituency influence. Those residuals were used in place of the standard measures in the second stages of their analyses.[5] None of the researchers found any substantive difference in their analyses, whether standard measures or residual measures were used.

Kalt and Zupan (1984) also developed a substitute measure for the standardized score that they called a "social issue" (SI) index. The SI index was based on each senator's vote on 34 "socio-ethical questions uncontaminated by pocketbook concerns" (p.289). Those issues included votes on increasing penalties for trafficking in child pornography, increasing the applicability of the death penalty, allowing immigration of communists, pardoning draft resisters, allowing disability payments to pregnant workers, and so on. Kalt and Zupan argued that members' voting on those issues could only reflect their personal ideologies; the SI index was very unlikely to be a proxy for constituencies' economic preferences regarding stripmining. For those unconvinced that even the SI index measured "personal" or "altruistic" ideology, Kalt and Zupan created a "residual" SI score for each senator. No matter how ideology was measured—by ADA score, residual ADA score, SI score, or residual SI score—the results of the analyses were virtually identical.

All tests of the validity of making inferences regarding personal ideology from standardized scores have come to the same conclusion: standardized scores do measure members' personal ideologies.

Inferring Preferences from Interviews with Representatives

All but one of the studies that have been done make inferences from constituency characteristics and other voting by representatives. To simplify presentation of the findings from those studies, and because issue area might influence findings (Clausen, 1973), those studies are grouped by general issue area in later discussion.

Because of the difficulty of getting interviews with representatives and the time required, only one study has obtained the data necessary for making inferences directly from the representatives themselves. Getting the data from representatives makes inferences more direct, especially regarding respresentatives' own ideologies. However, it decreases the sample of representatives that can be studied (as many representatives will not permit interviews of this type). Furthermore, there are validity problems with representatives' responses, as they may incorrectly evaluate constituencies' preferences and may feel compelled to give politically acceptable responses regarding either their own or their constituencies' preferences.

The one study that based inferences on responses by representatives was John Kingdon's (1973), *Congressmen's Voting Decisions.*

THE KINGDON STUDY

Kingdon interviewed members of Congress to find their own attitudes and their perceptions of their constituencies' attitudes regarding specific voting decisions. For each decision, he also asked about positions taken by fellow congressmen, by each member's staff, by interest groups, by party leaders, and by the administration. Kingdon could observe the behavior of members crosspressured by their constituencies and any other factor—including personal ideology.

Kingdon believed that a "consensus mode" dominated Congressional decisionmaking—that when deciding how to vote, members sought primarily to avoid controversy. Basically, Kingdon saw members as subject to a "field of forces," forces exerted by constituencies, personal attitudes, respected colleagues, party leaders, interest groups, their staffs, and the administration. When that field of forces had a concensus or near-concensus, as was most often the case, Kingdon argued that members almost always voted with the concensus.

Kingdon (p. 236) presented the data in Table 4–1 to show that his concensus mode operated.

Members generally, but not always, voted with their field of forces. However, even with just one or two forces out of line with the rest of the field, members occasionally voted with those forces. The relative power of the different forces can be estimated by noting which forces were

TABLE 4–1   Forces out of Line with the Field and Members' Voting Decisions

	Voted against the One	Voted with the One
One Force out of Line		
Interest Groups	22	0
Constituency	19	1
Administration	11	0
Party Leadership	5	0
Own Attitude	4	4
Fellow Congressmen	1	0
Staff	1	0
Two Forces out of Line		
Administration/Party Leadership	10	0
Constituency/Interest Groups	8	0
Interest Groups/Staff	4	0
Admistration/Interest Groups	3	0
Constituency/Party Leadership	2	0
Fellow Congressmen/Administration	1	0
Fellow Congressmen/Party Leadership	1	0
Interest Groups/Party Leadership	1	0
Own Attitude/Fellow Congressmen	0	5
Own Attitude/Constituency	0	1

Source: Kingdon, 1973: 236.

strong enough to cause members to vote against the rest of the field of forces.

There were 20 instances when members felt that their constituencies favored one vote, while all other pressures (including their own attitudes) favored a different vote. In only 1 of the 20 instances did a member bow to constituency pressure. In contrast, there were 8 instances when members' own opinions conflicted with all other pressures (including the position of the constituency). In half of those instances, members persisted in voting their own positions.

There were eleven decisions when members felt that their constituencies plus one other force favored one vote, while all other pressures favored a different vote. In only one of those decisions did a member vote with his constituency—the one time that the constituency's opinion happened to coincide with his or her own opinion. In contrast, there were six decisions when members' opinions of what votes were proper were supported by the position of only one other force. In every one of those decisions the members voted their own positions—including five decisions when members' positions were opposed to what they thought were the positions of their constituencies.

In total, there is very little evidence of constituency control. In the 43 decisions when constituency pressure was thought to be driving members one way and their own attitudes were driving them the other, members chose to vote with their constituencies only 5 times.

That is not to say there is no evidence of constituency *influence*. In the 60 decisions when members were not crosspressured by their constituencies, they always voted with their personal ideologies.

Constituency pressure was not as strong a factor in determining vote choice as was personal ideology, but members did bow to constituency pressure 12% of the time when it ran contrary to their own attitudes. In contrast, members never deviated from their own position when that position coincided with the position favored by the constituency.

Before turning to the other studies, it is worth highlighting the importance of personal attitude in determining members' votes. Of the 104 decisions that Kingdon examined, members voted their own opinion 99 times. They always voted their own opinion if the other forces in their field were not uniformly lined up against it. And if those forces were uniformly against, they still voted their own position half of the time.

In a revision of his original work, Kingdon (1981: 249) recognizes the strength of personal attitude in determining voting decisions when there is no concensus in the field of forces:

> ... the congressman prefers his own policy attitude unless he is pulled away from it under specified circumstances. Thus a high-priority request from a president of his own party or an intense constituency preference on a high-salience issue may overrule his own attitude. Short of those rather extraordinary circumstances, the legislator's goal of promoting his conception of good public policy carries the day.

Kingdon's research strongly suggests that representatives act virtually as free agents, voting their own opinions of what is best almost regardless of the pressures arrayed against them.

STUDIES BASED ON CONSTITUENCY CHARACTERISTICS AND MEMBER IDEOLOGY

Studies comparing the relative impact on congressional voting of constituency preferences (inferred principally from constituency economic characteristics) and members' ideology (inferred principally from standard ratings) are relatively new to political science. The first of those studies dates from 1974. Since that time there has been such a proliferation of those studies that it is impractical to review every one in this chapter. Because the overwhelming majority of those studies fit into three main policy areas where constituency control might be expected to be strong, the review that follows will cover the major studies in those three areas: defense and foreign policy, energy policy, and welfare and economic policy.

Voting on Defense and Foreign Policy

Conventional wisdom has held that representatives are particularly responsive to constituency interests in the defense area, scrambling to get defense contracts and bases. In fact, early commentators often dismissed defense issues as purely "real estate" questions (Dawson, 1962).

However, defense and foreign policy are issues that sharply divide members along ideological lines. And those issues are ones that constituents are not likely to know or care a great deal about. Consequently, members may be less willing to deviate from their own ideologies to vote constituency preferences in this policy area than they would be in other areas.

Four studies of voting in the defense and foreign policy area have now measured the strength of constituency influence once ideology is controlled. Those studies are discussed in detail below.[6]

The Bernstein and Anthony Study. The first study was by Robert Bernstein and William Anthony (1974). They studied Senate votes in 1968, 1969, and 1970 on whether to fund the anti-ballistic-missile (ABM) system. Their methodology was to treat the independent variables as dichotomies.

Based on standard ideological indices (ADA, ACA, and Conservative Coalition scores), Bernstein and Anthony classified each senator as liberal or conservative. The liberals were presumably ideologically pressured to oppose the ABM; the conservatives were presumably ideologically pressured to support the ABM.

Constituencies' economic benefits were inferred from research and development contracts that were to be awarded if the ABM were funded. Senators representing states that were to receive one million dollars or more in contracts or subcontracts were classified as constituency pressured to vote for the ABM. Senators representing states that were not to receive those contracts were classified as constituency-pressured to vote against the ABM because their constituents would be paying for the system without receiving a monetary return.

Senators' voting positions on the ABM issue were measured for each year. Guttman scales were constructed based on three votes in 1968, three in 1969, and two in 1970. Scale scores ran from 0, for least supportive of the ABM each year, to 3, for most supportive.

Treating the independent variables as dichotomies allowed Bernstein and Anthony to look directly at crosspressured senators for evidence of constituency control. Liberals representing states that would benefit economically and conservatives representing states that would suffer economically were crosspressured. They were forced to decide whether to vote their own beliefs or bow to constituency control.

Table 4–2 summarizes Bernstein and Anthony's (p. 1203) findings. The behavior of crosspressured senators is in boldface. The higher the index number, the more supportive of the ABM.

TABLE 4–2   Mean Position on the ABM and (Number) of Senators by Ideology, Party, and State Economic Benefit

	PARTY			
	REPUBLICAN		DEMOCRATIC	
Ideology	State Benefit	No State Benefit	State Benefit	No State Benefit
1968				
Conservative	2.91 (8)	**2.71** (20)	3.00 (7)	**2.87** (15)
Liberal	**1.60** (5)	1.33 (3)	**1.45** (11)	1.43 (28)
1969				
Conservative	3.00 (10)	**2.67** (21)	3.00 (5)	**2.92** (13)
Liberal	**1.33** (6)	1.33 (6)	**1.18** (11)	1.15 (27)
1970				
Conservative	3.00 (10)	**2.81** (21)	3.00 (5)	**2.88** (13)
Liberal	**0.50** (6)	1.00 (6)	**0.95** (11)	0.56 (27)

(3 = most pro-ABM position; 0 = most anti-ABM position)
Source: Bernstein and Anthony, 1974: 1203.

The table shows that liberals who represented states that would economically benefit did not desert their ideological position and vote for the ABM. In fact, the most anti-ABM position taken by any group was held by the Republican liberals in 1970 who represented states that would have benefitted from passage of the ABM. On a 0-3 scale of support for the ABM, the mean scores for liberals with economic incentives to vote for the ABM ranged from 0.5 to 1.6. The six comparisons that can be made show no consistent differences in voting between groups of liberal senators whose constituencies presumably were pushing for the ABM and groups of liberal senators whose constituencies were presumably not pushing for the ABM.

There is no more evidence of constituency control if one looks at the conservatives representing states that would not benefit economically. Just as liberals would not desert their ideological positions to get contracts for their constituencies, so conservatives would not desert their ideological positions to avoid having their constituencies pay for those contracts.

On the 0-3 scale of support for the ABM, conservatives whose constituencies would economically suffer if the ABM passed never averaged less than a 2.67. Conservatives representing states that would benefit showed slightly more support for the ABM than did those representing states that would not benefit, but the differences were never statistically significant.[7] There is no appreciable evidence of constituencies influencing the voting behavior of conservative senators. Almost all crosspressured conservatives voted the same as other conservatives.

Because voting on the ABM issue covered three years, Bernstein and Anthony had the opportunity to measure whether constituency influence varied over time. Senators might have thought they could "get away with" voting their ideological positions in 1968 without much fear of electoral effect, but then shifted to "playing it safe" as the spotlight of national publicity focused on the very close Senate votes of 1969 and 1970. Such a shift would suggest that constituencies eventually exercised control over their representatives, even though that control might not be apparent in any given year.

However, analysis of the actual voting behavior of crosspressured senators who served all three years showed no such shift. There were ten liberals who represented states that would receive economic benefits if the ABM passed and who could have shifted their votes over time to become more pro-ABM. Of the ten, only one did so. Five maintained their original positions, and four actually shifted to become more anti-ABM over time. There were twenty-nine conservatives representing states that would not benefit from ABM passage. Of those, only one moved to a more anti-ABM stance over time. Twenty-six maintained their original positions, and two shifted to a more pro-ABM position. Senators were not deserting their ideological positions to vote with their constituencies' economic interests; if anything, they were deserting their constituencies' interests to vote with their ideological leanings.[8]

To conclude, the Bernstein and Anthony study found no evidence of constituency control. Crosspressured liberals tended to vote the liberal position; crosspressured conservatives tended to vote the conservative position. There was virtually no evidence of crosspressured representatives bowing to constituency pressure in any given year or over the whole time period.

The Wayman Study.   Frank Wayman's (1983) study of how "doveish" senators were, was the first of the defense studies to treat the independent variables as continuous. In contrast to the Bernstein and Anthony study, his dependent variable dealt with defense voting generally, not with the adoption of a single weapons system. His use of continuous, rather than dichotomous, independent variables allowed him to search for even very slight shifts in voting that might be attributable to constituency influence.

Wayman used eleven 1977 votes to measure how doveish senators were. He used three separate measures of constituency benefit: Department of Defense (DOD) expenditures per capita; net gain or loss per capita from DOD expenditures and DOD tax burden; and net job gain or loss due to military spending per capita. He used ADA ratings to measure the liberalism of each senator.

Wayman used multiple regression analysis to test for whether the constituency variables had any influence on voting once ideology had been controlled. That is, after predicting votes purely on the basis of ideology, Wayman tested to see if the predictions could then be improved by using the additional information from the three constituency measures. Similarly, he tested to see whether ideology had any influence on voting once the constituency measures had been controlled.

Unfortunately, Wayman did not actually list the partial or multiple correlations that would tell us how responsive senators were to the different independent variables, controlling for the influence of the others. However, he did state (p. 29) that his multiple regression analyses showed

> that ideology (ADA rating) has a significant impact on the voting, and that the other variables do not. The effect of the economic variables is weak, not statistically significant (indeed, sometimes even in the 'wrong' direction).

Overall, Wayman's findings were not much different from those of Bernstein and Anthony. Both studies found that senators' voting on defense issues reflects their personal ideology. Neither study found evidence that constituency pressure, at least as measured by the money the "military-industrial complex" pours into each constituency, significantly affects the way in which that ideology is translated into votes.

The McCormick and Black Study. While the economic benefits to be derived from defense spending are perhaps the most obvious measures of constituency pressure in that area, it is useful to check one's findings by measuring constituency pressure in some other fashion. James Mc-Cormick and Michael Black (1983) were able to do that in their study of voting on the Panama Canal Treaties.

As McCormick and Black noted, polls during the six months prior to ratification of the treaty constantly showed over 60% of the public opposed to the treaties—yet they passed in the Senate by a vote of 68-32. Was nobody listening to his or her constituents?

McCormick and Black reasoned that if any senators were listening, they would be the ones up for reelection later that same year (1978). "Giving away the Canal" was sure to be an issue in reelection campaigns, so if senators were trying not to alienate their constituencies immediately before the election, they would be especially likely to vote against the treaties. Other senators, with reelection campaigns more than two years away, would feel much less constituency pressure to vote against the treaties.

McCormick and Black used ADA scores to measure ideology. They also controlled for region (Northeast, Midwest, Border, South, or West), party, and degree to which each senator tended to support the president's legislative program. They looked first at all senators voting on the treaties, then focused separately on those who announced their positions early and those who were "late deciders." They used standardized logit coefficients to measure the relative influence of each independent variable, controlling for all other variables. The logit coefficients are based on the odds that a category of senators will vote for or against the treaty. The larger the coefficient for a category of senators, the greater the odds that a senator falling in that category would oppose (if the coefficient is positive) or support (if the coefficient is negative) the treaties. McCormick and Black's results are presented in Table 4–3.[9]

If those up for reelection were feeling constituency pressure to vote against the treaties, it barely showed in their votes. The coefficients showed no statistically significant associations between senators' votes and whether they were up for reelections. Among the early deciders, those up for reelection were slightly more likely to oppose the treaties than were those not up for reelection. But among the late deciders, on whom one might expect constituency pressures to be the greatest, those up for reelection were slightly less likely to oppose the treaties than were those not up for election.

In contrast, the associations between ideology and voting were statistically significant for both early and late deciders. Liberals were significantly less likely to oppose the treaties than were conservatives.

TABLE 4–3   **Standardized Logit Coefficients between Opposition to the Panama Canal Treaties and Whether up for Reelection, Ideology, Region, Party, and Degree of Presidential Support: 1978**

	STANDARDIZED LOGIT COEFFICIENTS		
Variable	Whole Senate	Early Deciders	Late Deciders
Up For Reelection	1.21	1.12	-.46
Ideology (Liberalism)	-3.76*	-2.34*	-2.04*
Region			
Northeast	.99	-.15	1.71
Midwest	1.54	1.72	1.86
West	.01	.14	-1.19
Border	-.76	.16	-.16
South	-1.80	.08	-1.88
Party (Democratic)	-1.09	-.39	-1.49
Presidential Support	-.55	-.21	-.34

(* significant at the .05 level)
Source: McCormick and Black, 1983 in *Legislative Studies Quarterly*. Copyright © 1983 by Comparative Legislative Research Center.

McCormick and Black's finding were, therefore, very similar to the findings from the other defense and foreign policy studies. Senators tended to vote their ideologies, little influenced by their constituencies or any other factor.

The Fleisher Study. In the latest of the studies of voting on defense and foreign policy, Richard Fleisher (1985) combined the two methodological approaches discussed above to treat the independent variables as both dichotomous and continuous variables.

Fleisher studied five Senate votes on the B-1 bomber taken between 1975 and 1978. For the dichotomous analysis, Fleisher defined as high-economic-benefit states those which were among the top ten in B-1 spending or B-1 spending per capita. He used ADA scores to categorize senators as liberal or conservative. Table 4–4 summarizes his findings (p. 206); percentages for crosspressured senators are shown in boldface.

As with the ABM analysis, liberals representing high-benefit states and conservatives representing low-benefit states were crosspressured. Fleisher's results did, therefore, show some constituency influence on the senators' voting. Liberals motivated by constituency pressure to vote for the B-1 did so 36% of the time; liberals not so motivated voted for the B-1 only 13% of the time. Similarly, conservatives representing low-benefit states voted against the B-1 32% of the time, while those representing high-benefit states only voted against the B-1 11% of the time. While senators were not deserting in droves from their ideological preferences to vote their constituencies' economic interests, about 21-23% more were voting against their ideological positions when constituency pressure pushed them in that direction than were voting against their ideological positions when their constituencies were not pushing them.

Fleisher's dichotomous analysis did not find evidence of constituency *control* in the sense of a general willingness of senators to bow to constituency pressure. Senators were far more likely to vote on the basis of their own ideological preferences than they were to vote on the basis of the economic benefits for their constituents. Nevertheless, the dichotomous analysis did find some constituency *influence* on senators'

TABLE 4–4 Percentage Voting for the B-1 Bomber by Ideology and State Economic Benefit, 1975-78

	STATE ECONOMIC BENEFIT			
	High		Low	
Liberals	**36%**		13%	
(N)		(73)		(155)
Conservatives	89%		**68%**	
(N)		(44)		(169)

Source: Fleisher, 1985: 206.

voting, and that influence could be investigated in more detail by going to an analysis that treated the independent variables as continuous.

When treating the variables as continuous, Fleisher used discriminant function analysis to search for evidence of constituency influence on senators' positions on the B-1.[10] The size of the discriminant function coefficient measured the strength of association between the independent variable and how the senators voted on the B-1, controlling for the effects of other independent variables. Fleisher's results are reported in Table 4-5.

For only the earliest of the votes did Fleisher find statistically significant evidence of constituency influence. For the last two votes, when one might expect constituency influence to be greatest, the signs of the coefficients for state economic benefit were negative. Those negative signs indicated that once ideology was controlled, senators representing states that would receive the greatest economic benefits from passage of the legislation were actually somewhat more likely to vote against the B-1 than were senators representing states that would receive lesser economic benefits. Thus, the limited constituency influence uncovered in the dichotomous analysis appears to have occurred early, then dissipated.

In contrast, the ideological influence on voting was significant throughout the time period. That influence was strong regardless of whether the senators represented high-benefit states or low-benefit states.

Conclusion.   Studies of Senate voting on defense and foreign policy issues reveal very little evidence of constituency control. On occasion, especially early in the development of an issue, there is evidence that a relatively small number of senators do deviate from the positions suggested by their own ideologies to vote the positions favored by their constituencies. However, the predominant pattern is for senators to vote in accord with their own ideological preferences—even when that involves

TABLE 4–5   **Standardized Discriminant Coefficients Showing Influence of Ideology and State Economic Benefits on Senators' Support for the B-1: Five Votes**

Date of Vote	Ideology-H*	Ideology-L*	State Economic Benefit
6/5/75	.90**	1.63**	.71**
5/20/76	.97**	1.28**	.66
5/20/76	1.08**	1.45**	.23
7/18/77	1.28**	.85**	-.33
2/1/78	1.16**	.99**	-.39

(* Ideology-H = ideology for those representing high-benefit states; Ideology-L = ideology for those representing low-benefit states)
(** significant at .05 level)
Source: Fleischer, 1985.

voting against constituency preferences. That pattern is especially apparent as issues develop over time, when crosspressured senators are more likely to shift away from constituency toward ideological pressures, than they are to shift in the reverse direction.

Studies of Voting on Energy Policy

Constituency economic interests with respect to legislation on energy issues are so apparent, so strong, and so geographically concentrated that the energy issue area appears to be a likely place to find constituency influence. Furthermore, constituents are likely to have more interest in and a better understanding of the consequences of decisions on energy policy than of the consequences of decisions on defense and foreign policy. Members might expect that constituents would be less willing to defer to members' judgments on energy issues than on defense and foreign policy issues.

In addition, ideological divisions are not as fundamental on energy policy as on defense and foreign policy. There are ideological issues, including controlled versus free markets, small versus large producers, production versus conservation, but even prominent liberal and conservative economists have shown willingness to compromise on most of those issues. Members might feel less wedded to their own ideologies in the energy area than in the defense and foreign policy area.

With constituencies' preferences of greater consequence and ideological preferences of lesser consequence, one would expect studies of voting on energy policy to show greater constituency control than did studies of voting on defense and foreign policy.

There have been four studies of voting on energy issues for which one can judge the extent of constituency control or influence. Those are reviewed below. In general, they do show somewhat more constituency influence than the defense studies showed, but they show no clear evidence of constituency control.

The first of the studies was Edward Mitchell's (1979) analysis of House voting on natural gas deregulation. That was followed by Joseph Kalt's (1981) study of Senate voting on petroleum policy, Robert Bernstein and Stephen Horn's (1981) general analysis of energy voting in the House, and Joseph Kalt and Mark Zupan's (1984) study of Senate voting on the reclamation of strip mined lands.

The Mitchell Study. Mitchell looked at House voting on a 1976 bill that would deregulate natural gas. He argued that constituency support for deregulation tended to vary directly with (1) the amount of natural gas production in a producing district and (2) the percentage of natural gas supply that was curtailed by regulation to consuming districts. He further argued that because deregulation would raise prices, constituency opposition to deregulation would tend to vary directly with the percentage of homes in the district heating with gas. Once ideology and party were controlled, constituency influence could, therefore, be estimated from the associations between voting on deregulation and production, curtailment, and gas heating.

Mitchell treated the independent variables as continuous measures. He measured production by whether a member was from a gas-producing state. He measured curtailment by the percentage of the Federal Power Commission's "gas requirements" for each state that were cut off during the winter of 1975-76. He measured gas heating by the percentage of all occupied housing units in a state heated with utility gas in 1970 and by the average annual residential gas consumption per customer for 1970.[11]

Mitchell used a number of measures of ideology, including ADA and ACA scores. He also transformed ADA and ACA scores by a "probit function" that served to give almost all members more extreme liberal or conservative ratings than was the case with the standard ADA and ACA ratings. (All of his measures of ideology correlated very closely, and any one measure could be used in place of another without appreciably changing his findings.)

As control variables, Mitchell measured the percentage of population in urban areas, percentage of workers in white collar jobs, and members' percentage of the vote in 1974.

Mitchell used multiple regression analysis to determine the influence of each of the variables on congressional voting, controlling for the effects of all of the other variables. He used t-values from the regression analysis (p. 612) to distinguish the statistically significant from the statistically insignificant influences. Table 4–6 shows those t-values; values over 1.64 were significant.

The t-values showed that ideology and party were significantly related to voting on natural gas deregulation. One measure of constituency position, gas production, was also significantly related to voting. Controlling for ideology and party, representatives from gas-producing states were more likely to favor deregulation than were representatives from non-gas-producing states.

Mitchell compared the independent variables in terms of how well they predicted representative's votes. His summary (p. 604), quoted below, was the basis for his overall conclusion that only ideology was of any consequence in explaining representative's behavior:

1. Ideology alone predicts over ninety percent of the votes.
2. A Democratic congressman is somewhat more likely to vote against deregulation, but this connection is relatively weak—not one more congressional vote is correctly predicted when a party variable is added to the equation.
3. A congressman from a producing state is somewhat more likely to vote for deregulation, but this connection is also relatively weak—again, not a single additional vote is explained by this variable.

TABLE 4–6   T-Values for Multiple Regression of Various Independent Variables on Voting for Natural Gas Deregulation: 1976

Properties or Measures	T-Values
Constituency Influence	
Gas Production	2.2*
Gas Curtailment	1.1
Percentage Heating With Gas	.8
Average Residential Gas Consumption	-1.5
Ideology	
ADA	-4.4*
ADA Probit Function	-5.9*
Party (Democratic)	-3.8*
Urbanization	- .6
Percentage White Collar	- .8
Members' Percentage of Vote	.6

(* significant at .05 level)
Source: Mitchell, 1979: 612. Drawn from material published originally in 57 Texas Law Review 591-613 (1979). Copyright 1979 by the Texas Law Review. Reprinted by permission.

This pioneering study of House voting on energy policy showed much the same pattern evident in the studies of Senate voting on defense. Constituency influence was not irrelevant, but it was very weak in comparison to the influence of each representative's ideology.

The Kalt Study.   Mitchell's study shook up some of his fellow economists who were accustomed to thinking of members of Congress as surrogates for the economic interests of their constituencies. In fact, other economists were so accustomed to thinking that voting did and should reflect economic interests that they termed it "shirking" when a member voted his or her ideological preference rather than the economic interest of the constituency (Kalt, 1981; Kau and Rubin, 1982; Kalt and Zupan, 1984). One of those economists, Joseph Kalt (1981), studied Senate voting on petroleum policy to see whether the ideological influence found in the Mitchell study could be explained away as simply reflecting underlying constituency economic interests.

To rid his ideology measure of any possible reflection of economic interest, Kalt used the technique discussed earlier to create a "residual" measure of ADA based on the variation in ADA scores that could not be accounted for by 15 measures of constituency economic interests, a measure of constituency liberalism, or by each senator's political party affiliation.

Kalt used four measures of constituency economic interests. One, listed in Table 4–7 as "Crude," was a measure of the relative importance of crude oil production in each state. The second, listed as "Large

TABLE 4–7   T-Values from Logit Analysis Measuring the Significance of Ideological and Constituency Influence in Predicting the Probability of Pro-Crude Voting

Variables	T-Value
Residual ADA Measure	-16.96*
Constituency Influence	
Crude	5.21*
Large Refiner	- .93
Small Refiner	- .05
Energy Use	- 3.73*

(* statistically significant at the .05 level)
Source: Kalt, 1981: 267.

Refiners," was the value of shipments by large refiners in the state as a fraction of state income. The third, listed as "Small Refiners," was, similarly, the value of shipments by small refiners. The fourth, listed as "Energy Use," was total energy expenditures as a share of state personal income. Kalt argued that the first measure was an index of constituency support for legislation benefiting crude oil producers; the other three measures indexed constituency opposition to such legislation.

Kalt's dependent variable, the probability of voting for legislation benefiting crude oil producers, was based on 36 Senate votes between 1973 and 1977. As the independent and dependent variables were all treated as interval, Kalt selected a technique, logit analysis, that would relate variation in each of the independent variables to variation in the dependent variable while holding constant variation in each of the other independent variables. Table 4–7 presents the t-values from Kalt's logit analysis (p. 267). T-values above 1.64 indicate those variables that were statistically significant in accounting for the Senate voting.

Using the "residual" ADA measure did not explain away or even substantially weaken the statistical significance of ideology, which it would have done if ADA scores were, in large part, proxies for constituency influence.

Kalt did find evidence of significant constituency influence. The greater the importance of crude oil production to the state, the more likely a senator representing that state was to vote in favor of legislation benefiting the crude oil producers. In contrast, the greater the relative cost of energy use in a state, the less likely a senator representing that state was to vote in favor of that legislation.

However, senators were not responding exclusively to constituency influence. Their own ideologies were significant in determining their votes. The more liberal a senator, the less likely he or she was to vote for legislation benefiting crude oil producers.

Unfortunately, Kalt did not report the standardized logit coefficients that would allow a comparison of the relative impact of constituency and ideological motivations. The important substantive conclusions from his study thus were limited to two: (1) ideological motivation has ". . . a major impact on policy formation," but (2) ". . . ideology does not appear to be the only important explanatory variable" (p. 278).[12]

The Kalt and Zupan Study. Three years after the publication of his petroleum analysis, Kalt combined with Mark Zupan (1984) for a study of Senate voting on the Surface Mining Control and Reclamation Act (SMCRA). Their analysis was somewhat more detailed than the one Kalt had presented previously, but their methodological and substantive conclusions basically duplicated those of the petroleum study, with one important addition. While the Kalt study did not compare the relative strength of constituency and ideological influences, this study did. This is the only study of congressional voting to show constituency influence to be at least equal to that of ideology.

The SMCRA, signed into law in 1977, required the restoration of strip mined land to its premined state. The economic effects of the act were to (1) raise the cost of strip mining coal (raising the cost of coal mining for surface producers of coal), (2) raise the price of coal to the consumer, (3) make it more profitable to mine coal underground, and (4) reduce the cost to ranchers, farmers, lumberers, and recreationalists of using land that could be or had been strip mined. In addition, the act made for a more pleasant environment. Hence, the passage of the act hurt and benefited a number of different groups.

Kalt and Zupan looked to see how strong each of the groups were in each state. If constituencies were influencing congressional voting, they expected to find associations between group strength in the state and the voting of the senator from that state, once ideology was controlled.

There were 21 votes on the SMCRA or its vetoed predecessors. Kalt and Zupan, using a logit technique, combined those 21 votes into an index of opposition to strip mining (pro-SMCRA). That was the dependent variable in their analyses.

They used several variables to measure strength of constituency opposition to strip mining. For each state, those included measures of underground coal reserves as a fraction of state personal income, the agricultural and timber revenues of land that could be strip mined, the prospective value of land already stripped that would be reclaimed under the act, and the total membership in six environmental groups as a percentage of the voting-age population. In addition, they created measures estimating the concentration of interests among underground producers and among environmentalists.

Kalt and Zupan also had several measures of strength of constituency support for strip mining. For each state, those included measures of the average increase in cost of surface mining that would result from passage of the SMCRA, surface reserves of coal as a fraction of state personal income, and the percentage of electricity generated from coal. They also created measures estimating the concentration of interests among strip mine producers and among consumers.

Kalt and Zupan used a variety of measures of personal ideology. Those included each senator's League of Conservation Voters (LCV) rating (LCV ratings can be looked at as liberalism ratings on conservation issues), social issue (SI) index (based on each senator's vote on 34 "socio-ethical questions uncontaminated by pocketbook concerns" [p. 289]), a "residual" LCV measure, and a "residual" SI measure. As noted earlier, their results were nearly identical regardless of the measure used. For simplicity, Table 4–8, below, reports the results when the LCV ratings were used as the ideological measure.

Kalt and Zupan used standardized logit coefficients and t-values to determine the relative influence and statistical significance of each of the independent variables on opposition to strip mining, while controlling for the effects of all of the other independent variables. Their results (p. 288) are presented in Table 4–8.

Based on analysis of the t-values, the findings in Table 4–8 are similar to those in Table 4–7. Statistically significant associations are evident between ideology and voting and between some measures of constituency influence and voting.

However, the Kalt and Zupan study went beyond the Kalt study in presenting standardized coefficients. The standardized coefficients enabled comparisons of the strengths of association. Of the statistically significant coefficients, the value of reserves of underground coal in a

TABLE 4–8   Standardized Logit Coefficients and T-Values Showing the Influence of Various Independent Variables on Senators' Opposition to Strip Mining

Property or Measure	Standardized Coefficient	T-Value
Constituency Influences		
Underground Reserves	.73	2.37*
Concentration: Underground Producers	.03	.54
Agriculture and Timber Revenues	.12	1.40
Value of Stripped Lands	.22	3.30*
Environmental Group Membership	.00	.02
Concentration: Environmentalists	-.07	-1.14
Increase in Surface Mining Costs	-.22	-3.47*
Reserves of Surface Coal	-.57	-1.71
Concentration: Strip Mine Producers	.00	.07
% of Electricity Generated from Coal	-.13	-1.83
Concentration: Consumers	-.08	-1.29
Ideological Influence		
LCV Rating	.65	10.05*

(* = significant at the .05 level)
Source: Kalt and Zupan, 1984: 288.

state had a particularly strong effect on voting. The greater the value of underground reserves as a percentage of state income, the greater the opposition to strip mining by senators from that state. Personal ideology also had a very strong impact on voting: The more liberal the senator, the greater the opposition to strip mining.

The value of stripped land and the increase in surface mining costs resulting from the passage of the SMCRA had somewhat weaker effects on voting. The greater the value of stripped land in a state, the greater the opposition to strip mining by senators from that state; the greater the costs that would result from passage of the SMCRA, the greater the support for strip mining.

Thus, in contrast to the other studies of congressional voting, the Kalt and Zupan study found substantial constituency influence over representatives' voting. Because Kalt and Zupan did not treat the variables as dichotomous, they do not isolate crosspressured senators, and it is impossible to tell how often constituency influence was sufficient to cause senators to actually vote *against* their ideological preferences. In other words, it is impossible to tell whether constituency *influence* extended to constituency *control* on the issue of strip mining, but it may have.

The Bernstein and Horn Study. The Mitchell study of House voting estimated constituency economic characteristics from state characteristics. All of the other studies have been of Senate voting. Because it is much more difficult to get measures of constituency benefits or constituency attitudes for Congressional districts than for states, there have been very few studies of House votes that relied on district-level data. The first of those was a study by Robert Bernstein and Stephen Horn (1981) of energy voting in the House.

One might anticipate that studies of House voting would unearth greater evidence of constituency influence than would studies of Senate voting. Constituency economic benefits are likely to be more uniform and more important within a district than within a state. Similarly, constituency opinion is likely to be more decisively for or against any issue within a district than within a state. In spite of that, the Bernstein and Horn study found, as did the Mitchell study earlier, evidence of very little constituency influence on voting in the House.

Bernstein and Horn developed an index of opposition to legislation that would benefit major oil companies. Each member of the House was given a score equal to the percentage of his or her votes that opposed the major oil companies on five bills before the 94th Congress: one requiring a rollback of oil prices, one prohibiting joint ventures to develop energy sources on federal leases, one deregulating the price of natural gas for small producers only, one lifting price controls on diesel fuel and home heating oil, and one barring government assistance to private companies wishing to build uranium-enrichment plants.

The independent variables were treated both as dichotomies and as continuous variables. That allowed a search for both constituency control and for constituency influence. The ideology of representatives was measured by ADA scores. Constituency economic interest was measured by the amount of oil produced in each district. When treated as dichotomies, the ADA scores were coded as liberal or conservative; constituency influence was based on whether or not a House member represented an oil-producing district (OPD).

Table 4–9 shows the distribution of opposition to the oil companies by group, percentages for crosspressured members in boldface (p. 239).

TABLE 4–9   Percentage of Votes Opposed to the Oil Companies by Ideology and District Economic Benefits: 94th Congress

	DISTRICT ECONOMIC BENEFIT			
	Oil-Producing		NonOil-Producing	
Liberal	**80%**		86%	
(N)		(24)		(178)
Conservative	6%		**22%**	
(N)		(71)		(146)

Source: Bernstein and Horn, 1981: 239.

The most clearly crosspressured representatives were the liberals from OPDs. But there is only slim evidence that they bowed to constituency economic pressure: They averaged 80% opposition to the oil companies, only a trifle less than the 86% opposition that was registered by the liberals who represented nonoil-producing districts (NOPDs).

Conservatives representing NOPDs might also be viewed as crosspressured, as their oil-consuming constituents would have to pay for benefits (especially higher regulated prices) going to the oil companies. Some of the conservatives apparently did bow to economic pressure to oppose the oil companies. Conservatives representing NOPDs averaged 78% support for the oil companies, somewhat less than the 94% support shown by conservatives representing OPDs.

In sum, analysis of crosspressured representatives suggests that, at most, there was slight constituency influence, *not* constituency control. Representatives did not generally bow to constituencies' wishes. Liberals from OPDs voted more like liberals than like representatives of oil interests; conservatives from NOPDs voted more like conservatives than like representatives of oil consumers.

The weakness of constituency influence was highlighted in the analysis of the continuous variables. Bernstein and Horn used the parital r correlation coefficient to measure the effect of each independent variable on extent of opposition to the oil companies after controlling for the effects of all the other variables. Their results are shown in Table 4–10.

TABLE 4–10 Partial r Correlation Coefficients between Opposition to the Oil Companies and Ideology, Party, and Amount of Oil Produced: 94th Congress

Variable	Partial Correlation Coefficient
Ideology (Liberalism)	.77
Party (Republican)	-.39
Amount of Oil Produced	-.18

(all coefficients significant at .01 level)
Source: Bernstein and Horn, 1981: 240.

The -.18 between the amount of oil produced and opposition to the oil companies indicates a weak, but statistically significant, constituency influence. After controlling for the effects of ideology and party, the greater the oil production in the district, the lower the opposition to the oil companies by the representative from that district. However, members were not primarily voting constituency wishes. Constituency influence was much weaker than either party or ideological influence on congressional voting.

To visually depict the relative impact of constituency influence, Bernstein and Horn (p. 242) plotted regression lines showing the association between ideology (ADA scores) and opposition to the oil companies for Democrats, Republicans, those representing oil-producing districts (OPDs) and those representing nonoil-producing districts. Those plots are shown in Figure 4–1.

For all ADA values, Democrats showed quite a bit more opposition than did Republicans. "The smallest difference in projected scores show[ed] 10.7 percent more opposition by Democrats than by Republicans. Even that difference [was] statistically significant" (p. 241-42). Party affiliation affected the way in which members responded to their ideological inclinations.

In contrast, whether or not members represented oil-producing constituencies had virtually no effect on how they responded to their own ideological leanings. For almost all ADA value, representatives from OPDs tended to show less opposition to the oil companies than did representatives from NOPDs. However, the differences were very slight: "for no ADA rating [were] the projected opposition scores of the two groups separated by more than six percent, and the difference in projected scores [was] never statistically significant at the .05 level" (p. 241). Basically, members responded in the same way to their ideological inclinations regardless of the type of district they represented.

Conclusion. The studies of voting on energy issues showed varying amounts of constituency influence, but never constituency control. Regardless of how it was measured, the personal ideology of members always proved to be a strong and statistically significant factor in account-

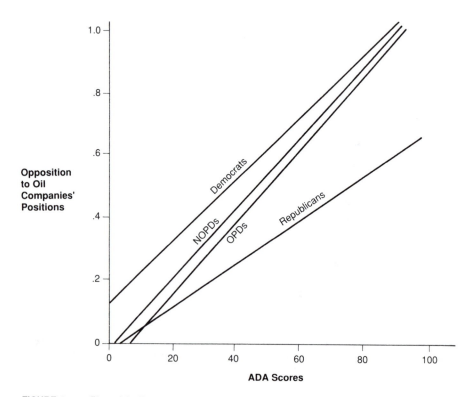

FIGURE 4–1   Plots of the Regression Lines of ADA vs. Opposition to the Oil Companies
Source: Bernstein and Horn, 1981: 242.

ing for Congressional voting behavior. There is evidence that members did not exclusively vote their own convictions, but they rarely ignored those convictions when they conflicted with the economic interests of their constituencies.

Overall, the evidence shows that members were more willing to deviate from their own ideological positions on energy issues than on defense issues. Perhaps that reflects (1) less clear ideological positions on energy issues than on defense issues, (2) greater constituency concern regarding energy issues than defense issues, or (3) a combination of the above.

Focusing just on the studies of voting on energy issues, comparisons of the determinants of voting in the two chambers showed that constituency influence could account for less of the variation in voting in the House than in the Senate. The direction of that difference is not what is suggested by differences in the homogeneity of House and Senate districts. However, it may reflect a greater expectation on the part of senators than representatives that citizens will know of them and their records, and also the greater threat of defeat in the Senate than in the

House. To the extent that the threat of electoral defeat causes any modification in members' behavior, that threat and modification would be greater in the Senate than in the House.

Studies of Voting on Welfare and Economic Policy

Welfare and economic policy are pocketbook issues for virtually all constituents. Taxation, family assistance, minimum wages, food stamps, and so on, are issues of immediate concern to large numbers of constituents. In contrast, building a weapons system or ratifying a treaty are issues of interest, but of no immediate concern to most constituents. Therefore, one might expect members of Congress to feel greater pressure from their constituents on welfare and economic issues than on defense and foreign policy issues.

However, welfare and economic policy are also issues on which there is sharp ideological division between liberals and conservatives. Ideological differences with respect to wealth transfers and government control of the economy are much more fundamental than are ideological differences with respect to strip mining and synthetic fuels. One might, therefore, expect members of Congress to feel greater ideological pressure on welfare and economic policy issues than on energy issues.

On defense and foreign policy issues, ideological pressure is intense; constituency pressure somewhat removed. Members rarely deviate from their ideological positions to vote with their constituencies; constituency influence is weak and fleeting. On energy issues, ideological pressures are somewhat weaker; constituency pressure a bit more immediate. Members, at least in the Senate, show greater willingness to deviate from ideological positions to vote with their constituencies; constituency influence may rival ideological influence. Welfare and economic issues fit between the other two types. Constituency and ideological influence are both strong. Under these circumstances, how often will members bow to the wishes of their constituencies?

Five studies report on the relative importance of constituency and ideological motivation in congressional voting on welfare and economic policy. The first was an analysis of tax egalitarianism by Chris Dennis (1978). That was followed by studies by Gillian Dean, et al. (1981), James Kau and Paul Rubin (1982), Chris Awalt (1986), and Michael McKnight (1986) regarding, respectively, voting on family assistance, minimum wages, food stamps, and social services.

The Dennis Study. Dennis examined Senate voting on 76 amendments to the Tax Reform Act of 1976 that would, if adopted, increase or decrease income inequality. He defined as pro-egalitarian the position on each amendment that would shift after-tax income away from families with incomes above the median and/or would shift after-tax income to families with incomes below the median. Senators were given egalitarianism scores based on the number of times they voted the pro-egalitarian position on the 76 measures.

Constituency preference was measured by the state median family income. If senators responded to constituency pressure, the poorer the state, the more egalitarian the senator's voting would be.

Ideology was measured by ACA scores, and Dennis controlled for the effects of party. He used partial r correlation coefficients to measure the influence of each of the variables on egalitarianism, controlling for the effects of the others. His results are shown in Table 4–11.

After ideology and party were controlled, there was no significant association between state median family income and the voting of senators representing those states. One might have expected tax egalitarianism to be the type of bread-and-butter issue on which representatives of poorer states would be squaring off against representatives of wealthier states, but there is no evidence that that was the case.

The Dean, et al., Study.   Gillian Dean, et al., (1981) tried to examine the effects of both constituency opinion and constituency economic benefit on senators voting on the 1972 proposed Family Assistance Program (FAP). It is generally assumed that constituency support follows economic benefit, but Dean believed that the two variables were not only separable but negatively associated on the FAP. The FAP would have tended to transfer money from the public in general to the poor in the poorest states. Public opinion polls, however, tended to show highest support for the FAP in the wealthier northeastern states, and highest opposition to it in the poorer southern states. Hence, some senators were subject to constituency crosspressures in addition to constituency-ideology crosspressures. Under those circumstances, one might expect very little constituency influence. And that is what their study found.

Dean measured each senator's support for the FAP by a scale based on three FAP votes. Dean estimated constituency opinion in each state from known population charactistics of the states and from public opinion polls showing extent of support by each of the population groups for programs like the FAP. She based her measure of net aggregate

TABLE 4–11   **Partial r Correlations between Tax Egalitarianism and Conservatism, Party, and State Median Income**

Variable	Partial r
Conservatism (ACA)	-.59*
Party (Republican)	-.33*
State Median Family Income	-.07

(* = significant at .05 level)
Source: Dennis, 1978: Table 1.

economic benefits on an economic simulation of direct and induced economic impacts. She used ADA ratings to measure ideology.

Dean used maximum-likelihood estimates from probit analysis to measure the impact of each independent variable controlling for the effects of the other variables. The maximum-likelihood estimates measure the extent to which an increase in the independent variable increased support for the FAP. The more positive the estimate, the more an increase in the independent variable would tend to increase support for the FAP. The more negative the estimate, the more an increase in the independent variable would tend to increase opposition to the FAP. The results of the Dean, et al., analysis (p. 349) are shown in Table 4–12.

Only ideology and party were statistically significant in influencing voting on the FAP. This would be consistent with Dean's interpretation that senators who are crosspressured by constituency opinion and constituency economic benefit are likely to fall back upon their ideology or party for guidance in voting. However, when Dean reworked her analysis, dividing the sample into those who were constituency crosspressured and those who were not, the reanalysis failed to show statistically significant constituency influence even for those who were not crosspressured.

Given the constituency crosspressures and the fact that liberal legislation was proposed by a Republican president, voting on the FAP might not have been representative of other Senate voting on welfare and economic issues. Whatever the reason, the evidence was clear: constituency influence was of little importance on that vote.

The Kau and Rubin Study. James Kau and Paul Rubin (1982) investigated the five House votes that raised the minimum wage between 1949 and 1974. Their findings were more in line with the expectation of significant, but modest, constituency influence.

They had three measures from which they could infer constituency position: the average hourly earnings in manufacturing, the percentage unionized, and the percentage black in each state.[13] Since minimum wage laws tend to protect high-income workers and especially union workers,

TABLE 4–12 Maximum-Likelihood Estimates of the Relative Influence of Various Independent Variables on Senate Voting on the FAP, 1972

Variable	Estimate
Constituency Opinion	.13
Net Aggregate Economic Benefit	- .86
Ideology (ADA rating)	1.18*
Party (Republican)	.53*

(*statistically significant at the .05 level)
Source: Dean, et al., 1981: 349. Copyright © 1981 by authors. Reprinted by permission of Sage Publications, Inc.

they argued that constituency support for the minimum wage would tend to vary directly with the average wage and extent of unionization in the state. Since minimum wage laws tend to create additional unemployment for blacks, they argued that constituency support for the minimum wage would tend to vary inversely with the percentage black in the state. Kau and Rubin used ADA scores to measure ideology and they controlled for party.

Like Dean, et al., they used maximum-likelihood estimates based on probit analysis to determine the relative influence of each of the independent variables, controlling for the effects of the others. Their maximum-likelihood estimates measured the extent to which an increase in the independent variable increased the probability of a vote for raising the minimum wage. The more positive the estimate, the greater the probability that an increase in the independent variable would lead to a vote to raise the minimum wage. The more negative the estimate, the greater the probability that an increase in the independent variable would lead to a vote against raising the minimum wage. Kau and Rubin's results (p. 59) are shown in Table 4–13.

Their results showed statistically significant constituency influence on all but the first vote. Representatives from higher-wage states were more likely to be supportive of raising the minimum wage than were representatives from lower-wage states. At least on the 1966 vote, representatives from states with higher percentages of blacks were significantly more likely to oppose raising the minimum wage than were representatives from states with lower percentages of blacks. However, no measure of constituency position was as strongly associated with voting as was the measure of ideology: the more liberal the representative, the more likely he or she was to support raising the minimum wage.

Since the Kau and Rubin analysis treated the variables as continuous, it is impossible to estimate how frequently crosspressured rep-

TABLE 4–13   Maximum-Likelihood Estimates of Relative Influence of Independent Variables on House Voting to Raise the Minimum Wage: 1949-1974

Property or Measure	MAXIMUM-LIKELIHOOD ESTIMATE				
	1949	1955	1961	1966	1974
Constituency Position					
Average Hourly Earnings	1.38	1.36*	1.45*	1.39*	1.48*
Unionization	1.23	1.21	1.17	1.22	1.18
Percent Black	-1.73	-1.61	-1.54	-1.67*	-1.60
Ideology (Liberalism)	1.77*	1.97*	1.97*	1.90*	1.90*
Party (Democratic)	-.02	-.15	-.14	-.09	-.08

(* = significant at .05 level)
Source: Kau and Rubin, 1982: 59.

resentatives deserted their ideological positions to vote as their constituencies would prefer. As ideology was the strongest factor influencing the vote every year, it seems unlikely that desertion was widespread. Thus, their analysis gives evidence of constituency influence, but not of constituency control. As expected, constituency influence, relative to the influence of ideology, does not appear to be as strong as it was on strip mining, but it is more substantial than it was on the defense and foreign policy issues.

The Awalt Study and the McKnight Study. The last two studies to be examined used very similar methodology to analyze House voting on welfare issues. While they dealt with different pieces of legislation, they came to virtually identical conclusions.

Chris Awalt (1986) examined the 1981 vote on whether to require food stamp recipients to pay part of the cost of their stamps. Michael McKnight (1986) examined three 1984 votes: reauthorization of the child nutrition program, reauthorization of the head start program, and an amendment to the hunger relief act to expand eligibility for the program. Both researchers dichotomized their dependent variables into pro-welfare and anti-welfare positions.

They also dichotomized their independent variables. Both used district wealth as a measure of constituency pressure, assuming that wealthier constituencies would be more opposed to welfare programs than would poorer constituencies. Both used standard scores to classify representatives as liberal or conservative.[14] Awalt used percentage black as a second measure of constituency influence, classifying districts as high-percentage black if over 25% of the population was black. He argued that blacks are more supportive of food stamp programs than are whites in similar economic circumstances. McKnight used percentage voting for Walter Mondale as his second measure of constituency influence, classifying districts as liberal if over 50% voted for Mondale. He argued that liberal constituencies would be more in favor of welfare programs than would other constituencies.

Since both researchers used dichotomous measures, it is possible to look directly at the behavior of crosspressured representatives. Table 4–14 reports the percentages voting pro-welfare by constituency and ideological classification, crosspressured members in boldface.

Looking across the rows, it is immediately clear that crosspressured liberals vote little differently than other liberals. On these issues, liberal representatives almost completely ignored constituency preferences to vote in support of welfare programs. In contrast, crosspressured conservatives generally showed some responsiveness to constituency preferences. Crosspressured conservatives showed significantly more support than did other conservatives in all comparisons except the one controlling for district ideology.

The Awalt study is unique among studies of congressional voting in

TABLE 4–14   Ideology, Constituency, and Percentage (and N) Voting Pro-Welfare: Awalt and McKnight Studies

Awalt Study

Ideology — CONSTITUENCY CHARACTERISTICS

	Wealthier	Poorer	High % Black	Low % Black
Liberal	**98%** (99)	100% (36)	100% (36)	**98%** (99)
Conservative	30% (128)	**56%** (127)	**65%** (54)	37% (201)

McKnight Study

Ideology — CONSTITUENCY CHARACTERISTICS

	Wealthier	Poorer	Liberal	Conservative
Liberal	**96%** (70)	93% (76)	96% (48)	**94%** (98)
Conservative	33% (83)	**49%** (104)	**41%** (17)	42% (170)

Sources: Awalt, 1986; McKnight, 1986.

showing sufficient constituency control over a group of representatives to move the majority of the group to support a position in opposition to their personal ideologies. The majority of conservatives representing poorer districts or districts with substantial black populations voted not to require the purchase of food stamps, while the majority of other conservatives voted for that requirement.

The findings in both studies that it was the conservatives who responded to constituency pressures does not suggest that conservatives are generally more responsive to the wishes of the people than are liberals. As the earlier studies showed, such was not the case on defense or energy issues. What it does suggest is that conservative ideology is not as unalterably anti-welfare as liberal ideology is pro-welfare. Even conservative representatives from wealthier districts, conservative districts, and districts with few blacks opposed welfare only 58-70% of the time.

The greater percentage differences within columns than across rows reveals that for the House as a whole, ideological differences were stronger determinants of voting on these issues than were constituency differences.[15] However, constituency influence on conservatives was substantial enough or ideological influence weak enough so that constituency preference, not ideological preference, was the prime determinant of voting for crosspressured conservatives on at least one issue.

Conclusion.   The studies of voting on welfare and economic policy show a great deal of variation in the amount of constituency control or influence that is evident. Dennis (1978) and Dean, et al. (1981), found virtually no evidence of constituency influence. Kau and Rubin (1982) found substantial constituency influence. And Awalt (1986) and McKnight (1986) found substantial constituency influence over conservatives. On average, voting on welfare and economic policy is probably more responsive to constituency preferences than on defense or foreign policy, but perhaps not as responsive as voting on energy policy.

SUMMARIZING THE EVIDENCE

This chapter has reviewed virtually all of the available evidence regarding the extent to which constituencies control or influence the voting of their representatives. There is virtually no evidence of constituency *control*, that is, no evidence that members of Congress generally bow to the wishes of their constituencies when those wishes are contrary to the personal preferences of the members. There is some evidence of constituency *influence*, that is, evidence that controlling for ideology, representatives' support for a policy tends to vary directly with constituency support for the policy.

On virtually every issue, the prime determinant of Congressional voting is the personal ideology of the representative. On issues when ideological divisions are sharp and constituency preferences and knowledge are likely to be weak, such as on defense and foreign policy issues, ideology is virtually the only determinant of voting. As ideological divisions weaken and constituency preferences strengthen, for example, on some energy, welfare, or economic issues, members are more likely to deviate from their own positions and adopt those of their constituencies.

Overall, it is much more consistent with the evidence to view members of Congress as free agents, rather than as agents of their constituencies. As free agents they may take into account constituency preferences, but they are not controlled by those preferences.[16]

THEORIES OF WHY MEMBERS OF CONGRESS VOTE AS THEY DO

Let's step back a moment to consider what has been written on the general question of why members of Congress vote as they do. As Arthur Maass (1973) argues, the dominant trend in the literature is to treat members as though they had virtually no "free agency," that is, to assume that members' decisions are the results of external forces. Interest groups, party leaders, the president, wealthy contributors, constituents, and so on, are seen pushing the member one way or the other; the member's vote is the result of all the crosspressures. It's almost as though members of Congress are seen as objects in a physics laboratory; they have no volition, they simply move in accordance with the force diagram.

In laying out his theory of Congressional voting, Morris Fiorina (1974: 122) specifically states that "the representative . . . is not a free agent." And, in what must be the most explicit use of the physics analogy, James Kuklinski and Donald McCrone (1981) actually present a force diagram, complete with the representative depicted as a dot and force arrows labeled party and constituency pushing the dot in different directions.

To the extent that members of Congress are seen as making their own decisions, the dominant trend in the literature is very cynical with respect to the motives for those decisions. How often are members accused of voting for more spending in order to improve their reelection prospects? Yet, as Payne (1986) points out, such a view suggests that members are willing to jeopardize the prosperity of the country to achieve personal success.

Mayhew's (1974) discussion of "the electoral connection" is among the most cynical. He suggests that members use legislative voting to claim credit for benefits and to advertise positions on policies—regardless of whether those benefits and policies are put in place and regardless of whether the benefits and policies are desirable—simply to increase their own prospects for reelection.

One searches in vain through most of the modern classics on Congressional voting for even the suggestion that members consider such questions as whether policies are "proper," "just," or "good for the country."[17]

The myth of constituency control fits well in this dominant approach towards Congressional voting. Fundamentally, the myth contends that members of Congress are not free to vote as they think best. Instead, the desire for reelection and the fear of antagonizing constituents are seen as forces driving the member to vote as his or her constituents wish.

The evidence presented in this chapter shows that constituencies do not control Congressional voting. On issues from military spending to taxation, from energy policy to "giving away" the Panama Canal, members often turn down economic payoffs for their constituencies and vote against public opinion when their own ideologies tell them it is right to do so.

The dominant approach to explaining Congressional voting—much of it theoretically rather than empirically based—is wrong. The evidence shows that members of Congress are people, not dots in the center of force diagrams. By and large, they are people voting for what they think is best. There is no evidence that they are willing to sell out their principles or the well-being of their nation for extra protection at the ballot box. Members of Congress have their own views of whether policies are good or bad and they tend to vote on the basis of those views.

NOTES

[1] Erikson's (1978) reanalysis of the Miller-Stokes data is not included, although it might have been. Validity questions regarding both Erikson's measure of constituency position and Miller and Stokes' measure of members' perceptions of constituency position suggest that it is very risky to draw any conclusions from that study. Erikson found virtually no direct constituency influence in any of the three issue areas he examined. He found moderate associations between members' perceptions of constituency position and voting in two areas. But even in these areas, the indirect path from constituency to vote via members' perceptions was extremely weak.

Vedlitz's (1983) analysis of voting on gun control legislation and Kau and Rubin's (1982) analysis of voting on urban issues are not treated in this chapter because they fall outside of the three main issue areas. Garnham's (1977) analysis of congressional support for Israel is excluded because support for Israel is not a key tenet of conservative or liberal ideology. The findings of all three of those studies are consistent with the findings of most of the studies that are treated here: Ideology has the strongest impact on voting, but there is also significant constituency influence on congressional voting.

[2] Some have argued that a single conservative/liberal dimension is too insensitive to show the full effects of personal ideology, that we need to use different conservative/liberal dichotomies for different issue areas. These studies generally do use just a single-dimensional measure. However, the effects of personal ideology are sufficiently apparent using the single dimension that no more sensitive scale is necessary to make the point. Additionally, in the most detailed study to date of the ideologies of members of Congress, Jerrold Schneider (1979: 195) established that ideology is basically "unidimensional": "being strong, moderately, or not at all liberal in one policy dimension corresponds very highly with being liberal or conservative to the same degree in all of the other dimensions." Schneider's work was confirmed for the post-1970 period by Smith (1981).

[3] Concerns about whether voting-based measures of ideology really measure the personal ideologies of members of congress are raised most strongly by Peltzman (1984). His argument that members' "public" ideology is simply a surrogate for economic interests in their districts and not a reflection of their personal beliefs is not well supported by the data or arguments he presents. His basic contention is that if the economic characteristics of states or of senators' supporters within states correlate highly with ADA scores, then what others have been calling ideology (and measuring with ADA scores) is not the personal beliefs of the senators but a behavior forced upon them by the state economic interests they represent. That contention is based on the fallacy that coincidence shows causation. Even if he found a perfect association between ADA and economic characteristics, it would not mean that senators adopted the positions they did because of economic pressures.

Of course he does not find a perfect association. Thirteen economic variables seem to combine to account for 59% of the variance in ADA. However, eight of the thirteen variables are not significantly related to ADA by any accounting. Of the remaining five, the strongest association is between log of median family income and ADA—and the direction of that association suggests that senators are voting the opposite of their constituents' interests, as there is a positive association between income and ADA. The associations between ADA and race and urbanization also run in the wrong direction.

One might expect the poor, minorities, union workers, labor organizations, and so on to support more liberal senators once they find out their ideologies. That would suggest some correlation between constituency characteristics and voting. It would not mean that senators could not have and vote their own ideologies. What is most surprising is that in making the best case he can for the influence of constituency economic variables, Peltzman can find so many weak or misdirected associations.

[4] Those indicators included, for each state, the percentage nonwhite, the years of average voter education, the percentage urban, the percentage unionized, per capita personal income, the percentage of labor and property income from agriculture, the percentage of labor and property income from manufacturing, the percentage blue collar, the percentage white collar, the average voter age, the percentage of the vote going to McGovern, a measure of the importance of crude oil production, the value of large refinery shipments, the value of small refinery shipments, and energy expenditures as a share of personal income.

[5] For an argument that the residual ADA variable does not measure what social scientists or the general public usually mean by the term ideology, see Bernstein (1985).

[6] All of the studies also compared the relative strength of *bivariate* (uncontrolled) associations between voting behavior and both ideology and constituency economic interests. All found ideology to have much greater influence than constituency.

[7] Bernstein and Anthony used analysis of variance to test for significance. Their results (p. 1203) are shown below. Constituency pressure never had a significant impact on the voting:

Analysis of Variance in Position on the ABM Issue: 1968-1970

Source of Variance	F-RATIO		
	1968	1969	1970
Main Effects			
Ideology (I)	33.47*	85.54*	125.66*
Economic Benefit (E)	0.40	0.46	0.00
Party (P)	0.00	0.00	0.00
Interaction Effects			
I X E	0.00	0.00	0.26
I X P	0.08	0.62	0.00
P X E	0.08	0.15	1.32
I X E X P	0.00	0.15	1.45

(* significant at .01 level)

[8] Scores of 1 and 2 in 1968 were considered the equivalent of 1-1/2 in 1970.

[9] For a brief explanation and defense of the use of the logit coefficients, see Mc-Cormick and Black (1983).

[10] The discriminant function analysis was not reported in the published article, but in an earlier draft of that article.

[11] Estimating district characteristics from state characteristics may have weakened or strengthened the apparent constituency influence.

[12] Kalt does further analysis in which he constrains the coefficients in a variety of ways. For example, because a dollar of crude oil production produces roughly five times the value added as does a dollar of refinery shipments, he constrains the crude oil and refinery coefficients so that they are in the ratio of roughly 5:1. If that constraint is added, or other similar constraints, the refinery coefficients will be significant. But the ideology coefficient and its t-value is little affected.

[13] Estimating district characteristics from state characteristics may have weakened or strengthened the apparent constituency influence.

[14] The two authors used different cutoff points on district wealth and different standard liberalism ratings.

[15] All ideological differences are statistically significant at the .05 level.

[16] This study does not test the hypothesis that senators shift to more moderate positions as elections approach. That hypothesis has been suggested as evidence that senators are not free agents. The tests of that hypothesis that have been done have shown mixed and misleading results with small samples (Elling, 1982; Thomas, 1985; Wright and Berkman, 1986; Bernstein, 1988). A full test of the hypothesis may show some evidence of constituency influence but the shifts that have been evident so far are too weak (in the order of 7 ACA rating points in 3 years) to indicate constituency control.

[17] An exception is Kingdon's (1981) revision of his classic (1973) study.

FIVE

Summary, Conclusions, and Beyond

This book began with Robert Weissberg's (1976: 170) statement of what most people see as the primary function of elections:

> ...elections are seen as the primary mechanism through which common citizens control their government. Elections are, supposedly, the means by which leaders gone astray are replaced by ones more attuned to popular desires.

The evidence presented throughout the book suggests that this common view, called here the myth of constituency control, is incorrect with respect to members of Congress. Members who have "gone astray" are rarely replaced, and if they are replaced because they have gone astray, it is unlikely that the "common citizen" is doing the replacing. Elections do not serve as a "mechanism through which citizens *control* their government."

SUMMARIZING THE EVIDENCE

Evidence regarding the limited truth behind the myth of constituency control begins with observation of constituent behavior. Underlying the myth are assumptions regarding the behavior of constituents: that they know who the incumbents are; that they are aware of what the incumbents' policy positions have been; and that they reward and punish incumbents based on how far the incumbents' policy positions have differed from their own preferences. The evidence is, however, that probably less than a third of all constituents can recognize who their representatives are and what policy positions they have generally taken—and even that third tends not to evaluate incumbents on the basis of policy distance.

The assumptions regarding constituents do apply to a minority within any constituency. Knowledgeable constituents constitute almost half of those who vote, and while they tolerate a range of deviation from their own policy preferences, some of them can be provoked to retaliate against representatives who have deviated substantially—provided that they have reason to think that alternative representatives would have deviated by less. Knowledgeable voters are apparently aware that a Republican alternative probably would have been to the right of their Democratic representative and that a Democratic alternative probably would have been to the left of their Republican representative; consequently, they tend to punish Democrats who have deviated substantially to the left of their own preferences and Republicans who have deviated substantially to the right. They do not punish incumbents when there is no reason to expect that an alternative candidate would have been any closer to their preferences than the incumbent has been.

Thus, there *is* a group of voters behaving as the myth would project. However, it is a small group within the typical constituency, and incumbents, especially House incumbents, tend to win by wide margins. Consequently, those constituents who behave as the myth would suggest are rarely decisive in determining the outcome of reelection races.

The general inability of the knowledgeable, policy-evaluative minority to decide elections is further confirmed by analyses of the behavior of constituencies as aggregates. Three independent analyses could find no support for the hypothesis that incumbents' reelection probabilities varied inversely with their policy distance from their constituencies.

There is evidence that constituencies do not entirely ignore the policy positions taken by their representatives. Support was found for two hypotheses relating policy distance and reelection probability for specific types of elections: (1) in general elections, the further Republican incumbents have deviated to the right and Democrats have deviated to the left of their constituencies' preferences, the lower the probability of their reelection; (2) in primary races, the further Republican incumbents have deviated to the left and Democrats have deviated to the right of their constituencies' preferences, the lower the probability of their winning the nomination. Voters responding to policy deviation are sufficiently widespread and sufficiently knowledgeable about the relative positions of alternative representatives in the general elections and the primaries to affect the percentage of the vote that a constituency gives to an incumbent.

However, support for the two hypotheses must be kept in perspective: Little of the variation in the percentage of the vote given to incumbents is accounted for by extent of deviation from the constituencies' preferences. Extent of policy deviation is rarely decisive in general elections and almost never decisive in primaries.

Neither the analysis at the level of the individual constituent nor the analysis at the constituency level is able to discover more than a handful of races in either 1980 or 1984 when an incumbent's loss was probably the result of policy deviation. More importantly, neither analysis can discover more than another handful of races in which winning incumbents would have been defeated even if they had deviated by substantially more than they actually did.

The most telling evidence regarding the limited truth underlying the myth is found in observing the behavior of representatives. The occasional punishments meted out by constituencies *could be* sufficient to enforce general obedience by representatives to the wishes of their constituencies. However, a review of virtually all studies of members crosspressured by conflicting constituency and personal preferences shows that members do not generally bow to the wishes of their constituencies, but vote their own preferences instead.

The extent to which Congressional voting can be accounted for by the personal preferences of the members varies with the issue area. However, studies comparing the relative impact of personal preference, constituency preference, and other variables on the voting behavior of representatives and senators show that on virtually every issue, the primary determinant of Congressional voting is the personal ideology of the representative.

Overall, it is more consistent with the evidence to view members of Congress as free agents than as agents under the control of their constituencies. Constituencies tend to grant members considerable latitude on policy issues without punishing them at the polls. Members can generally afford to vote for what they think is right without expecting that their votes will cost them a seat in Congress; indeed, they tend to vote their own ideological beliefs, and such voting rarely does cost them, regardless of constituency opinion on the issues.[1]

THE FUNCTION OF ELECTIONS IN INFLUENCING POLICY

While there is little evidence that constituencies can *control* their representatives' policy positions, there is some evidence that they can *influence* those positions. Some of that influence may be attributable to limited responsiveness by representatives to pressures of reelection; more of that influence is probably attributable to the policy congruence between representatives and constituencies that results from the use of elections to make the initial selection of representatives.

Responsiveness to Reelection Pressures

Evidence that representatives may be influenced by reelection pressures is found in the generally positive correlations between members' support and constituencies' support for policies *after controlling* for the ideologies of the members. Further evidence that representatives may be responding to reelection pressures is found in the subordination by some crosspressured members, on virtually every issue, of their own ideological preferences to those of the constituencies. Still more evidence that representatives may be influenced by reelection pressures is the finding that members tend to shift their voting in the direction of the ideological preference of their new constituencies when their districts have been altered by redistricting (Glazer and Robbins, 1985).

This evidence of constituency influence must be kept in perspective: the responsiveness by members is quite limited. First, after controlling for ideology, the correlations between constituencies' support and members' support are quite weak. Second, only a minority of crosspressured members are generally willing to subordinate their own preferences to those of their constituents. And third, the ideological shifts by those representing altered districts are very slight.

Even that limited responsiveness may not be the consequence of having to face reelection. However, there seems to be enough truth to the myth of constituency control to encourage occasional acquiescence of representatives to the preferences of constituencies. After all, there are some citizens in every constituency who judge incumbents on the basis of policy distance, and occasionally those citizens are decisive in a reelection race. That members' voting is not simply reflective of their own preferences, but is occasionally responsive to constituencies' wishes, suggests that the threat of future rewards and punishments gives constituencies some influence over policy.

Policy Congruence and Initial Selection

Constituency influence over policy flows from more than the somewhat doubtful threat of electoral retaliation; it flows from the constituencies' initial selections of who their representatives will be. As Kingdon (1973: 46) states, "Different districts simply recruit people of different attitudes to run for Congress." The attitudes of most members tend to reflect the attitudes of those who selected them. For example, the correlation between the liberalism of the constituencies and the liberalism of their representatives for 1984, as measured in Chapter 3, is .61. When members vote their own beliefs, they tend to be voting the beliefs of their constituencies. That members' attitudes sometimes conflict with those of their constituencies, and that *in those instances* they tend to vote against their constituencies, should not obscure the fact that *most of the time* their attitudes do not conflict with those of their constituencies and they, therefore, vote as their constituencies want them to. Members don't *have* to adopt the positions of their constituencies; they, however, often *choose* to adopt them.

Changes in constituencies and representatives over time may cause their attitudes to diverge (Stone, 1980). The impact of initial selection in prompting policy congruence fades over time, and the limited responsiveness to reelection pressures may not be enough to maintain congruence at its initial level. But the average tenure of members of Congress is under 11 years (Glazer and Grofman, 1987); the election of a new representative tends to reestablish the coincidence between constituency and representative opinion.

Influence and Representation

As was noted in Chapter 2, responsiveness by representatives to constituency influence may mean responsiveness to unrepresentative minorities. Responsiveness resulting from reelection pressures is responsiveness to minorities within the constituencies that have sufficient knowledge of and interest in incumbents' policies to threaten retaliation at the polls. Even responsiveness resulting from initial selection is responsiveness to the minorities within the constituencies that voted, and more especially, voted on the basis of policy preferences in that initial election.

The policy preferences of knowledgeable and interested minorities may not be representative of the policy preferences of entire constituencies. The atypical socioeconomic distribution among knowledgeable, policy-evaluative minorities suggests that their policy preferences are probably different from those of other constituents. The policy preferences of knowledgeable, policy-evaluative minorities are especially likely to be unrepresentative in primary contests preceding the initial selection of representatives, as the electorates in those contests tend to favor more extreme ideological positions than are characteristic of the constituencies as a whole (Aranson and Ordeshook, 1972; Coleman, 1972; Bernstein, 1976; Wright, 1978; Wright and Berkman, 1986).

Thus, elections serve to promote limited constituency influence, but that limited influence may not make government policy more responsive to the wishes of the people as a whole. Only to the extent that the interested minorities are representative of the public as a whole does the limited influence exerted by those minorities encourage government responsiveness to the policy preferences (good or bad) of the public.

INCREASING CONSTITUENCY INFLUENCE

Whether constituencies, or more specifically, knowledgeable and interested minorities within constituencies, *should* have greater influence over government policy than they do now, is a question that cannot be answered by the type of analysis in this book. Whether constituencies are *likely* to increase their influence beyond what it is now, is a question that can be addressed based on the factors that have been treated above.

Increasing Policy Congruence

The major source of constituency influence appears to be policy congruence, and policy congruence tends to decrease with time since initial selection of the representative. Thus, a decrease in the average tenure of representatives would tend to increase constituency influence. However, the prospects for a future decrease in the average tenure are not particularly good.

Looking back over the past 35 years, there is no clear trend in the average tenure for members of Congress (Ornstein, et al., 1984). With reelection probabilities over .91, it is unlikely that members will be forced to shorten their tenures. Any decrease in average tenure would have to come from a shift toward earlier retirement.

John Hibbing (1982) notes that there is a factor encouraging such a shift: the "increasing time demands" of Congressional service and the "resultant familial sacrifices." James Payne (1977a; 1980a) and John Rhodes (1976) suggest a second factor: increasing inclinations among members to seek higher office. Either increasing desire to escape from public life or increasing desire for higher office could lead members to resign their seats after shorter tenures than have been traditional.

However, Payne's (1980a) work also discloses a factor that will tend to increase tenure: the long-term trend for members to enter Congress at a younger age. The younger entry age (the median is now well under 40) means much longer tenures by members before they have to retire because of infirmities associated with advanced age.

Overall, it is hard to project with any confidence a decrease or increase in the average tenure of members. There is, therefore, no reason to project a marked increase in constituency influence over government policy as a consequence of a decrease in tenure.

Increasing Reelection Pressures

A second source of constituency influence appears to be the reelection pressures facing members of Congress. The responsiveness of members to such pressures would presumably increase with an increase in size of the knowledgeable, policy-evaluative minorities in their constituencies. However, the prospects for an increase in the size of those minorities are not good.

Despite increases in campaign spending, C-SPAN broadcasts, and efforts by political action committees (PACs), the media, interest groups, the League of Women Voters, and so on, there is no evidence that knowledge of incumbents and their policies is becoming more widespread. As the data in Chapter 2 show, there has been no long-term increase in the proportion of the population who can recognize their representatives.

It seems reasonable to conclude that the current deficiency in knowledge is not a result of the information being unavailable. The deficiency is more likely the result of what are seen as high opportunity costs to the citizen of receiving and retaining policy-relevant information.

To receive and retain policy-relevant information about incumbents, citizens have to divert time from more immediately rewarding pursuits—business, family, entertainment, and so on. For most citizens, the costs in lost opportunities are apparently too high to pay.

The increasing pressures and diversions of modern life do not suggest that the opportunity costs of receiving and retaining policy-relevant information will be declining in the near future. Thus, there is no reason to project increased constituency influence resulting from an expansion of knowledgeable, policy-evaluative minorities.

MYTH AND REALITY

As detailed in the Introduction, the myth of constituency control over Congress permeates the textbooks and articles on elections, representation, and Congressional behavior. Whatever the reasons for its acceptance—from the theories that it ought to work, to the comfort derived from thinking that it does—the *evidence* is that the myth is largely untrue.

The myth exaggerates and distorts the influence that constituencies have in determining government policy. It exaggerates the influence that constituencies have over their representatives' policy stances and distorts the point in the electoral process where that influence is the strongest. Constituencies do not control the policies adopted by their representatives; they have some influence over what those policies are, but members are by and large free to adopt what they think best. Constituency influence does not flow primarily from electoral threats against those in office, but rather from the initial selection of representatives. Once selected, liberals are likely to adopt liberal policies and conservatives to adopt conservative policies. The desire for reelection has only marginal impact in shifting members from ideological preferences should those preferences differ from the preferences of their constituencies.

In addition to exaggerating and distorting the role of the constituency, the myth demeans the role of members. At best, it suggests a constituency-input, policy-output model of Congress in which members' thoughts and deliberations are irrelevant. At worst, it suggests a Congress of unprincipled vote-seekers who deliberately ignore what they believe best for the nation in order to improve their own reelection prospects. There is little evidence that those views accurately reflect how voting decisions are made by members of Congress.

The myth of constituency control is not a harmless folk tale to be passed on to future generations of students. It fundamentally misstates the relationship between the constituency and the representative. It is time for writers and researchers to refrain from perpetuating an essentially incorrect view of how representative government functions in the United States.

NOTES

[1] This conclusion is based on findings from many independent studies of different types of data at different levels of analysis. Those findings are consistent in showing that members of Congress can and do vote as they wish with only slight risk of punishment at the polls. However, estimation of the risk involved is based on analyses of single reelection races, and even a slight risk may build over time. Additional research is necessary to define more clearly the extent of risk that *over a career* is associated with different degrees of deviation from the policy preferences of the constituency.

If the probability of winning successive reelection races is constant, as suggested by Amihai Glazer and Bernard Grofman (1987), the probability of winning a given number of consecutive races is the probability of winning a single race raised to the power of the given number. For example, if the probability of winning a single race is .92, then the probability of winning 5 consecutive races is $(.92)^5 = .66$, and the risk of losing somewhere along the line is .34. The exponential decrease in the probability of winning means that even if being a certain distance from the constituency's preferred policy position increases the risk of losing a single reelection race only slightly, the cumulative effect over a hoped-for career is to raise the risk of losing by a great deal. For example, if deviation drops the probability of winning a single reelection race to .88 from .92, it raises the risk of defeat before being reelected 5 times from .34 to .47.

But the probability of winning successive reelection races may not be constant for those a given distance from the constituency's policy preference. It may be that if one wins reelection one or more times at a given distance from the constituency's policy preference, then the probability of reelection becomes equal to the probability for those who do not deviate at all. Only research on the effect of deviation over time can clarify the risks involved.

References

ABRAMOWITZ, ALAN (1980). "A Comparison of Voting for U.S. Senator and Representative in 1978." *American Political Science Review*, 74, pp. 633-40.

ACHEN, CHRISTOPHER (1977). "Measuring Representation: Perils of the Correlation Coefficient." *American Journal of Political Science*, 21, pp. 805-815.

ARANSON, PETER AND PETER ORDESHOOK (1972). "Spatial Strategies for Sequential Elections." In Richard Niemi and Herbert Weisberg, eds., *Probability Models of Collective Decision Making*. (Columbus: Charles Merrill.)

AWALT, CHRIS (1986). "Conscience and/or Constituency: Congressional Voting Behavior on the Food Stamp Program." Unpublished Paper. (College Station, TX: Texas A&M University.)

BARONE, MICHAEL AND GRANT UJIFOSA (1980-1986). *The Almanac of American Politics*. (Washington: Publisher varies with year.) (Douglas Matthews coauthors in 1980.)

BERELSON, BERNARD, PAUL LAZARSFELD, AND WILLIAM MCPHEE (1954). *Voting: A Study of Opinion Formation in a Presidential Campaign*. (Chicago: University of Chicago Press.)

BERNSTEIN, ROBERT (1976). "A Simple Spatial Model of Voting with Teaching Applications." *Teaching Political Science*, 3, pp. 347- 372.

BERNSTEIN, ROBERT (1985). "Comment on Carson and Oppenheimer." *American Political Science Review*, 79, pp. 824-825.

BERNSTEIN, ROBERT (1988). "Do Senators Moderate Strategically?" *American Political Science Review*, 82, pp. 237-241.

BERNSTEIN, ROBERT AND WILLIAM ANTHONY (1974). "The ABM Issue in the Senate, 1968-1970: The Importance of Ideology." *American Political Science Review*, 68, pp. 1198-1206.

BERNSTEIN, ROBERT AND JAMES DYER (1984). *An Introduction to Political Science Methods*, 2nd edition. (Englewood Cliffs, N. J.: Prentice-Hall.)

BERNSTEIN, ROBERT AND STEPHEN HORN (1981). "Explaining House Voting on Energy Policy: Ideology and the Conditional Effects of Party and District Economic Benefits." *Western Political Quarterly*, 34, pp. 235-245.

BIRCH, ANTHONY (1971). *Representation*. (New York: Praeger.)

BOND, JON (1985). "Perks and Competition: The Effects of District Attention over Time." A paper presented to the Midwest Political Science Association Meetings in Chicago, April 17-20.

BOND, JON, CARY COVINGTON, AND RICHARD FLEISHER (1985). "Explaining Challenger Quality in Congressional Elections." *Journal of Politics*, 47, pp. 510-524.

CAMPBELL, ANGUS, GERALD GURIN, AND WARREN MILLER (1954). *The Voter Decides*. (Chicago: Row-Peterson.)

CARSON, RICHARD AND JOE OPPENHEIMER (1984). "A Method of Estimating the Personal Ideology of Political Representatives." *American Political Science Review*, 78, pp. 163-178.

CENTER FOR POLITICAL STUDIES, UNIVERSITY OF MICHIGAN (1978-1984). *American National Election Studies*. (Ann Arbor, Mich.: Inter-University Consortium for Political and Social Research.)

CLAUSEN, AAGE (1968-69). "Response Validity: Vote Report." *Public Opinion Quarterly*, 32, pp. 588-602.

CLAUSEN, AAGE (1973). *How Congressmen Decide: A Policy Focus*. (New York: St. Martin's.)

CLOTFELTER, JAMES (1970). "Senate Voting and Constituency Stake in Defense Spending." *Journal of Politics*, 32, pp. 979-983.

CNUDDE, CHARLES AND DONALD MCCRONE (1966). "The Linkages between Constituency Attitudes and Congressional Voting Behavior: A Causal Model." *American Political Science Review*, 60, pp. 66-72.

COBB, STEPHEN (1976). "Defense Spending and Defense Voting in the House: An Empirical Study of an Aspect of the Military Industrial Complex." *American Journal of Sociology*, 82, pp. 163-182.

COLEMAN, JAMES (1972). "The Positions of Political Parties in Election." In Richard Niemi and Herbert Weisberg, eds., *Probability Models of Collective Decision Making*. (Columbus, OH: Charles Merrill.)

CONGRESSIONAL QUARTERLY (1979-1985). *CQ Weekly Report*. (Washington, D.C.: Congressional Quarterly Press.)

CONVERSE, PHILIP (1964). "The Nature of Belief Systems in Mass Publics," in David Apter (ed.), *Ideology and Discontent* (New York: Free Press.)

COVER, ALBERT AND DAVID MAYHEW (1981). "Congressional Dynamics and the Decline of Competitive Congressional Elections." In Dodd and Oppenheimer (eds.), *Congress Reconsidered*, 2nd ed. (Washington, D.C.: Congressional Quarterly Press, pp. 62-82.)

DAHL, ROBERT (1970). *After the Revolution? Authority in a Good Society*. (New Haven, Conn.: Yale University Press.)

DAWSON, RAYMOND (1962). "Congressional Innovation and Intervention in Defense Policy: Legislative Authorization of Weapons Systems." *American Political Science Review*, 56, pp. 46- 50.

DAVIDSON, ROGER AND WALTER OLESZEK (1981). *Congress and Its Members*. (Washington, D.C.: Congressional Quarterly Press.)

DAVIS, DAVID (1978). *Energy Politics*, 2nd ed. (New York: St. Martins.)

DAVIS, OTTO, MELVIN HINICH, AND PETER ORDESHOOK (1970). "An Expository Development of a Mathematical Model of the Electoral Process." *American Political Science Review*, 64, pp. 426-448.

DENNIS, CHRIS (1978). "The Revenue Side of Budgetary Politics: The Impact of Ideology on the Tax Reform Act of 1976." A paper presented at Southwestern Political Science Association meetings in Dallas.

DEAN, GILLIAN, JOHN SIEGFRIED, AND LESLIE WARD (1981). "Constituency Preference and Potential Economic Gain: Cues for Senate Voting on the Family Assistance Plan." *American Politics Quarterly*, 9, pp. 341-356.

DE TOCQUEVILLE, ALEXIS (1831). *Democracy in America*. (New York: New American Library, 1956.)

DIXON, ROBERT (1968). "Representation Values and Reapportionment Practice: The Eschatology of 'One Man, One Vote.'" In Pennock and Chapman, pp. 167-198.

DOWNS, ANTHONY (1957). *An Economic Theory of Democracy*. (New York: Harper & Row.)

ELLING, RICHARD. (1982). "Ideological Change in the U.S. Senate: Time and Electoral Responsiveness." *Legislative Studies Quarterly*, 7, pp. 75-92.

ENGLER, ROBERT (1964). *The Politics of Oil*. (Chicago: University of Chicago Press.)

ERIKSON, ROBERT (1971). "The Electoral Impact of Congressional Roll Call Voting." *American Political Science Review*, 65, pp. 1018-1032.

ERIKSON, ROBERT (1978). "Constituency Opinion and Congressional Behavior: A Reexamination of the Miller-Stokes Representation Data." *American Journal of Political Science*, 22, pp. 511-535.

ERIKSON, ROBERT AND GERALD WRIGHT (1985). "Voters, Candidates, and Issues in Congressional Elections," in Lawrence Dodd and Bruce Oppenheimer, eds., *Congress Reconsidered*, 3rd ed. (Washington, D. C.: Congressional Quarterly Press, pp. 87-108.)

EULAU, HEINZ, JOHN WALKE, WILLIAM BUCHANAN, AND LEROY FERGUSON (1959). "The Role of the Representative: Some Empirical Observations on the Theory of Edmund Burke." *American Political Science Review*, 53, pp. 742-756.

FENNO, RICHARD, JR. (1977). "U.S. House Members in Their Constituencies: An Exploration." *American Political Science Review*, 71, pp. 883-917.

FENNO, RICHARD, JR. (1978). *Home Style: House Members in Their Districts*. (Boston: Little, Brown.)

FEREJOHN, JOHN (1977). "On the Decline of Competition in Congressional Elections." *American Political Science Review*, 71, pp. 166-177.

FIORINA, MORRIS (1974). *Representatives, Roll Calls, and Constituencies*. (Lexington, KY: D. C. Heath.)

FIORINA, MORRIS (1977a). "The Case of the Vanishing Marginals: The Bureaucracy Did It." *American Political Science Review*, 71, pp. 177-181.

FIORINA, MORRIS (1977b). *Congress: Keystone of the Washington Establishment*. (New Haven, Conn.: Yale University Press.)

FIORINA, MORRIS (1981). *Retrospective Voting in American National Elections*. (New Haven, Conn.: Yale University Press.)

FLEISHER, RICHARD (1985). "Economic Benefit, Ideology, and Senate Voting on the B-1 Bomber." *American Politics Quarterly*, 13, pp. 200-211.

FREEDMAN, STANLEY (1974). "The Salience of Party and Candidate in Congressional Elections: A Comparison of 1958 and 1970." In Luttbeg (1981), pp. 118-122.

FROMAN, LEWIS (1963a). *Congressmen and Their Constituencies*. (Chicago: Rand McNally.)

FROMAN, LEWIS (1963b). "Inter-Party Constituency Differences and Congressional Voting Behavior." *American Political Science Review*, 57, pp. 57-61.

GANT, MICHAEL AND DWIGHT DAVIS (1984). "Mental Economy and Voter Rationality: The Informed Citizen Problem in Voting Research." *Journal of Politics*, 46, pp. 132-153.

GARNHAM, DAVID (1977). "Congressional Support for Israel: Voting Correlates in the 93rd Congress." A paper presented to the International Studies Association Meetings in St. Louis, March 16-20.

GLAZER, AMIHAI AND BERNARD GROFMAN (1987). "Two Plus Two Plus Two Equals Six: Tenure in Office of Senators and Representatives, 1953-1983." *Legislative Studies Quarterly*, 12, pp. 555-564.

GLAZER, AMIHAI AND MARC ROBBINS (1985). "Congressional Responsiveness to Constituency Change," *American Journal of Political Science*, 29, pp. 259-273.

GROSS, DOUGLAS AND JAMES GARRAND (1984). "The Vanishing Marginals, 1894-1980." *Journal of Politics*, 46, pp. 224-237.

HAMILTON, LEE (1987). "How a Member Decides." In Roger Davidson and Walter Oleszek, eds., *Governing*. (Washington, D.C.: Congressional Quarterly Press, pp. 227-230.)

HIBBING, JOHN (1982). "Voluntary Retirement from the U.S. House: The Costs of Congressional Service." *Legislative Studies Quarterly*, 7, pp. 57-74.

HINCKLEY, BARBARA (1976). "Issues, Information Costs, and Congressional Elections." *American Politics Quarterly*, 4, pp. 131-152.

HURLEY, PATRICIA (1982a). "Collective Representation Reappraised." *Legislative Studies Quarterly*, 7, pp. 119-136.

HURLEY, PATRICIA (1982b). "Electoral Change and Policy Consequences: Representation in the 97th Congress." A paper presented at the Southern Political Science Association meeting in Atlanta.

HURLEY, PATRICIA AND KIM HILL (1980). "The Prospects for Issue-Voting in Contemporary Congressional Elections: An Assessment of Citizen Awareness and Representation." *American Politics Quarterly*, 8, pp. 425-448.

JACOBSON, GARY (1987). *The Politics of Congressional Elections*, 2nd ed. (Boston: Little, Brown.)

JOHANNES, JOHN AND JOHN MCADAMS (1981). "The Congressional Incumbency Effect: Is It Casework, Policy Compatibility, or Something Else? An Examination of the 1978 Election." *American Journal of Political Science*, 25, pp. 512-542.

JOHANNES, JOHN (1984). *To Serve the People: Congress and Constituency Service*. (Lincoln: University of Nebraska Press.)

JONES, BRYAN (1981). "Reply to Adams and Ferber." *Journal of Politics*, 43, pp. 208-211.

KALT, JOSEPH (1981). *The Economics and Politics of Oil Price Regulation: Federal Policy in the Post-Embargo Era*. (Cambridge: MIT Press.)

KALT, JOSEPH AND MARK ZUPAN (1984). "Capture and Ideology in the Economic Theory of Politics." *American Economics Review*, 74, pp. 279-300.

KAU, JAMES AND PAUL RUBIN (1982). *Congressmen, Constituents, and Contributors: Determinants of Roll Call Voting in the House of Representatives*. (Boston: Martinus Nijhoff.)

KENNEDY, JOHN (1956). *Profiles in Courage*. (New York: Harper & Row.)

KINGDON, JOHN (1973). *Congressmen's Voting Decisions*. (New York: Harper & Row.)

KINGDON, JOHN (1981). *Congressmen's Voting Decisions*, 2nd ed. (New York: Harper & Row.)

KORCHIN, SHELDON (1946). *Psychological Variables in the Behavior of Voters*. Doctoral Dissertation, Harvard University.

KUKLINSKI, JAMES AND DONALD MCCRONE (1981). "Electoral Accountability as a Source of Policy Representation." In Luttbeg (1981), pp. 320-340.

LARSON, STEPHANIE (1987). "Does Learning about a Congressman's Voting Affect Evaluations of Him Despite a Successful Home Style?" A paper presented to the American Political Science Association Meetings in Chicago, September 3-6.

LAZARSFELD, PAUL, BERNARD BERELSON, AND HAZEL GAUDET (1948). *The People's Choice*, 2nd ed. (New York: Columbia University Press.)

LOCKERBIE, BRAD (1986). "Marginality-Homogeneity and Responsiveness Revisited." A paper presented to the Southern Political Science Association Meetings in Atlanta, November 5-8.

LUTTBEG, NORMAN (1981), editor. *Public Opinion and Public Policy: Models of Political Linkage*, 3rd ed. (Itasca, Ill: F. E. Peacock.)

MAASS, ARTHUR (1983). *Congress and the Common Good*. (New York: Basic Books.)

MACNEIL, NEIL (1963). *Forge of Democracy: The House of Representatives*. (New York: David McKay.)

MACRAE, DUNCAN, JR. (1976). *Dimensions of Congressional Voting: A Statistical Study of the House of Representatives in the Eighty-First Congress*. (New York: Octagon.)

MADISON, JAMES (1787). Federalist #51, *The Federalist Papers*. (New York: New American Library of World Literature, 1961.)

MANN, THOMAS AND RAYMOND WOLFINGER (1980). "Candidates and Parties in Congressional Elections." *American Political Science Review*, 74, pp. 617-632.

MARKUS, GREGORY (1974). "Electoral Coalitions and Senate Roll Call Behavior: An Ecological Analysis." *American Journal of Political Science*, 18, pp. 595-607.

MAYHEW, DAVID (1974). *Congress: The Electoral Connection*. (New Haven, Conn.: Yale University Press.)

McCormick, James and Michael Black (1983). "Ideology and Voting on the Panama Canal Treaties." *Legislative Studies Quarterly,* 8, pp. 45-63.

McCrone, Donald and James Kuklinski (1979). "The Delegate Theory of Representation." *American Journal of Political Science,* 23, pp. 278-300.

McCrone, Donald and Walter Stone (1986). "The Structure of Constituency Representation: On Theory and Method." *Journal of Politics,* 48, pp. 956-975.

McKnight, Michael (1986). "A Study of the Influences on Congressional Voting Behavior." Unpublished Paper. (College Station, TX: Texas A&M University.)

Mill, John Stuart (1860). *Considerations on Representative Government.* (New York: E. P. Dutton: 1951.)

Miller III, J.C. (1969). "A Program for Direct and Proxy Voting in the Legislative Process." *Public Choice,* 7, pp. 107-113.

Miller, Warren and Donald Stokes (1963). "Constituency Influence in Congress." *American Political Science Review,* 57, pp. 45-56.

Mitchell, Edward (1979). "The Basis of Congressional Energy Policy." *Texas Law Review,* 57, pp. 591-613.

Moyer, Wayne (1973). "House Voting on Defense: An Ideological Explanation." In Bruce Russett and Alfred Stepan, eds., *Military Force and American Society.* (New York: Harper and Row, pp. 106-142.)

Niemi, Richard and Herbert Weisberg, eds. (1976). *Controversies in American Voting Behavior.* (San Francisco: W. H. Freeman.)

Oppenheimer, Bruce (1974). *Oil and the Congressional Process.* (Lexington, KY: D. C. Heath.)

Ornstein, Norman, Thomas Mann, Michael Malbin and John Bibby (1984). *Vital Statistics on Congress, 1984.* (Washington, D.C.: American Enterprise Institute.)

Parker, Glenn (1980). "The Advantage of Incumbency in House Elections." *American Politics Quarterly,* 8, pp. 449-464.

Parker, Glenn (1987). "The Role of Constituent Trust in Congressional Elections." A paper presented to the American Political Science Association Meetings in Chicago, September 3-6.

Payne, James (1977a). "The Changing Character of American Congressmen: Some Implications for Reform." A paper presented at the Midwest Political Science Association Meetings in Chicago.

Payne, James (1977b). "The Democratic Paradox." *National Review,* July 21: 88-90, 109.

Payne, James (1980a). "The Personal Electoral Advantage of Incumbents," 1936-1976. *American Politics Quarterly,* 8, pp. 465- 482.

Payne, James (1980b). "Show Horses and Work Horses in the U.S. House of Representatives." *Polity,* 12, pp. 428-456.

Payne, James (1982). "The Rise of Lone Wolf Questioning in House Committee Hearings." *Polity,* 14, pp. 626-640.

Payne, James (1986). "Inside the Mind of a Big-Time Spender." *Reason,* 17 (July), pp. 41-44.

Payne, James, Oliver Woshinsky, Eric Veblen, William Coogan, and Gene Bigler (1984). *The Motivation of Politicians.* (Chicago: Nelson-Hall.)

Peltzman, Sam (1984). "Constituent Interest and Congressional Voting." *Journal of Law and Economics,* 27, pp. 181-210.

Pennock, J. Roland (1968). "Political Representation: An Overview." In Pennock and Chapman (1968), pp. 3-27.

Pennock, J. Roland and John Chapman (1968). *Representation.* (New York: Atherton Press.)

Pitkin, Hanna (1967). *The Concept of Representation.* (Berkeley: University of California.)

Pomper, Gerald (1980). *Elections in America: Control and Influence in Democratic Politics,* 2nd ed. (with Susan Lederman). (New York: Longman.)

Random House, (1967). *The Random House Dictionary of the English Language.* (New York: Random House.)

Ray, Bruce (1981). "Defense Department Spending and Hawkish Voting in the House of Representatives." *Western Political Quarterly,* 34, pp. 439-446.

RHODES, JOHN (1976). *The Futile System: How to Unchain Congress and Make the System Work Again.* (McLean, Va: EMP.)

RUSSETT, BRUCE (1970). *What Price Vigilance? The Burdens of National Defense.* (New Haven, Conn.: Yale University Press.)

SCHNEIDER, JERROLD (1979). *Ideological Coalitions in Congress.* (Westport, Conn.: Greenwood Press.)

SHANNON, W. WAYNE (1968). *Party, Constituency and Congressional Voting: A Study of Legislative Behavior in the United States House of Representatives.* (Baton Rouge, LA.: Louisiana State.)

SMITH, STEVEN (1981). "The Consistency and Ideological Structure of U.S. Senate Voting Alignments, 1957-1976." *American Journal of Political Science,* 25, pp. 780-795.

STOKES, DONALD AND WARREN MILLER (1962). "Party Government and the Saliency of Congress." *Public Opinion Quarterly,* 26, pp. 531- 546.

STONE, WALTER (1980). "The Dynamics of Constituency: Electoral Control in the House." *American Politics Quarterly,* 8, pp. 399- 424.

SULLIVAN, JOHN AND ROBERT O'CONNOR (1972). "Electoral Choice and Popular Control of Public Policy: The Case of the 1966 House Elections." *American Political Science Review,* 64, pp. 1256-68.

THOMAS, MARTIN (1985). "Election Proximity and Senatorial Roll Call Voting." *American Journal of Political Science,* 29, pp. 96-111.

TURNER, JULIUS (1951). *Party and Constituency: Pressures on Congress.* (Baltimore, Md.: Johns Hopkins.)

VEDLITZ, ARNOLD (1983). "The Relevance of Indirect Indicators in Assessing Constituency-Legislative Linkage: Gun Control 1968 and 1972." *Political Methodology,* 9, pp. 159-170.

WAYMAN, FRANK (1983). "Arms Control and Strategic Arms Voting in the U.S. Senate: Patterns of Change, 1967-1982." A paper presented to the International Studies Association Meetings in Mexico City, April 5-9.

WEISSBERG, ROBERT (1976). *Public Opinion and Popular Government.* (Englewood Cliffs, N. J.: Prentice-Hall.)

WEISSBERG, ROBERT (1981). "Have House Elections Become a Meaningless Ritual?" In Luttbeg (1981), pp. 341-353.

WHITBY, KENNY AND TIMOTHY BLEDSOE (1986). "The Impact of Policy Voting on the Electoral Fortunes of Senate Incumbents." *Western Political Quarterly,* 39, pp. 690-700.

WRIGHT, GERALD, JR. (1977). "Constituency Response to Congressional Behavior: The Impact of the House Judiciary Committee Impeachment Votes." *Western Political Quarterly,* 30, pp. 401-410.

WRIGHT, GERALD, JR. (1978). "Candidates' Policy Positions and Voting in U.S. Congressional Elections." *Legislative Studies Quarterly,* 3, pp. 445-464.

WRIGHT, GERALD, JR. AND MICHAEL BERKMAN (1986). "Candidates and Policy in United States Senate Elections." *American Political Science Review,* 80, pp. 567-590.

ZEIGLER, HARMON AND HARVEY TUCKER (1980). *Professionals Versus the Public.* (New York: Longman.)

Index

G

Gant, Michael, 19, 29, 31
Garnham, David, 95
General vs. primary elections (*see* Primary vs. general elections)
Glazer, Amihai, 101–2, 105
Grofman, Bernard, 102, 105

H

Hamilton, Rep. Lee, xiii–xiv
Hibbing, John, 103
Hill, Kim, 14, 31, 38
Hinich, Melvin, xiv, 31
Home style, 7, 36
Horn, Stephen, 77, 83–86
House vs. Senate (*see* Senate vs. House)
Hurley, Patricia, 14, 31, 37–38, 62

I

Ideology, (*see* Policy, Measurement)
Incumbents, (*see* Alternative representation, Change over time, Crosspressured representatives, Decisiveness of positioning, Delegates, Desire for reelection, Free agents, Initial selection, Measurement, Motivation of incumbents, Policy agreement, Policy congruence, Policy deviation, Policy positioning, Primary vs. general elections, Recognition of the incumbent, Reward and punishment, Shifts in position, Tenure)
Influence vs. control (*see* Control vs. influence)
Initial selection of representatives, 101–4
Issue areas:
conservation, 46, 58, 77, 81–83
defense and foreign policy, 13, 42, 46, 58, 62, 69–73, 75–77,

79, 86–87, 91, 93–95
energy policy, 46, 58, 62, 69, 77–85, 87, 91, 93, 95–97
legal rights, 38, 41–42, 44–45
welfare and economic policy, 41–45, 87–91, 93–95

J

Johannes, John, 4, 14–15, 31, 34–35, 39–41, 49, 57
Jones, Bryan, 65

K

Kalt, Joseph, 65–66, 77, 79–83, 97
Kau, James, 66, 79, 87, 89–90, 93, 95
Kennedy, John, 1, 10
Kingdon, John, 7, 60, 67, 69, 97, 101
Knowledge, 2–6, 8–9, 11–18, 20–23, 25–31, 50, 56, 94, 99, 102–4
Kuklinski, James, 61, 94

L

Larson, Stephanie, 4, 7, 36
League of Conservation Voters, 58, 82
League of Women Voters, 104
Likes and dislikes, 19–20, 29
Lockerbie, Brad, 37
Luttbeg, Norman, xvi, 7

M

Maass, Arthur, xvi, 7, 61, 94
MacNeil, Neil, xiv
MacRae, Neil, 62
Madison, James, xi, xiii
Mann, Thomas, 14, 30, 103
Margin of victory, 3, 26–29, 34–35, 41, 47–48, 54–55, 99
Mayhew, David, 1, 10, 94
McAdams, John, 14–15, 31, 34–35,